The Adventures of Dofesaba II 2019 & 2020 From Port Leucate to Lagos in Portugal

From May 19th to Sept. 16th 2019 And July 21st to Sept 12th 2020 (or "The Punic Coast Adventure" as well as "The Covid Year")

PETER J BELL

AuthorHouse™ UK
1663 Liberty Drive
Bloomington, IN 47403 USA
www.authorhouse.co.uk
UK TFN: 0800 0148641 (Toll Free inside the UK)
UK Local: 02036 956322 (+44 20 3695 6322 from outside the UK)

This book is printed on acid-free paper.

ISBN: 978-1-6655-8351-0 (sc)
ISBN: 978-1-6655-8350-3 (e)

Print information available on the last page.

Published by AuthorHouse 01/19/2021

Contents

About the Author v

Foreword by George Trevelyan CB. Captain of Cruising RLym YC. vii

Dedication ix

Preface xi

Acknowledgements xiii

Glossary of Terms in order of appearance xv

Chapter 1   Leaving France 1

Chapter 2   One month later. 2

Chapter 3   Arriving in Catalonia. 5

Chapter 4   Towards the bigger towns 10

Chapter 5   Cruising without a powered dinghy to Barcelona 14

Chapter 6   Off to Tarragona 18

Chapter 7   Peniscola and Westwards 24

Chapter 8   Canet de Berenguer & Valencia 27

Chapter 9   Valencia to Alicante 32

Chapter 10   Alicante to Cartagena 39

Chapter 11   Cartagena to Cabo de Gato 49

Chapter 12   Cabo de Gato to Benalmadena 56

Chapter 13   Escaping the Virus 67

Chapter 14   Arriving in Estepona 71

Chapter 15 Leaving Gibraltar and Orcas 77

Chapter 16 Cadiz and Puerto Sherry 83

Chapter 17 Mazagon and El Rompido 86

Chapter 18 To Isla Christina and Ayamonte 91

Chapter 19 Leaving Spain 95

Chapter 20 Leaving Spain - Again 104

Chapter 21 Isla Culatra - Vilamoura 106

Chapter 22 The Final Stretch 110

Glossary of Terms in Alphabetical order 119

About the Author

Peter Bell and his wife Mary came to sailing late in the day. Both were Scout Leaders and brought their family up to love the outdoors and to be self-sufficient. Peter was a Mountain Leader in Snowdonia until the rules changed and his body stopped working well enough to go up and down. Mary decided he needed a new hobby, on the flat, and so they went cruising on flotillas in Greece. After 3-4 years they bought Dofesaba – a Southerly 110 and two years later upgraded to the S42 RST – in their opinion, the pride of the fleet. In the mean time Peter did Day Skipper, Trans Channel course and Yacht Master Theory exams. Since then, up to 2021 they have 'Cruised' over 9000 miles, with many Adventures. Like many mature couples mostly retired they have used their summers 'wisely' Having taken their boat down the Canals du Midi during 2018, they then proceeded "Home" around Spain stopping at most of the Ports and harbours on their way, trying to satisfy Peter's quest for the culture and architecture of the Roman period, and his need for a decent sail and adventure. Mary just wanted to stay cool.

Peter and Mary live in Lymington are Members of the RLymYC often. Peter has been known to give lectures on his yearly adventures.

Foreword by George Trevelyan CB.
Captain of Cruising RLym YC.

Peter Bell is a phenomenon in his own lifetime. Years spent exercising his geophysical skills in the pursuit of hydrocarbons have, in some mysterious way, helped him to develop into a formidable navigator; and like many seamen, he likes to tell a tale. He likes to make a difference too. In this case, he has brought our attention to the joys of sailing the Punic Coast - and in giving it that name, he reveals another aspect of his character: his understanding of the effects of geological time, which has morphed into an understanding of the long history of all the coasts he sails along. He can see in them the cooling crusts of ancient rock, their subsequent metamorphoses, and finally in archaeological and historical time, he is in touch with the varied peoples and cultures which have inhabited, farmed, invaded and defended them. Especially defended: there is no Fort or Citadel along these coasts he has not visited and analysed. He is at home with Iberians, Phoenicians, Greeks, Romans, Normans, Moors, Crusaders, Conquistadores - and he loves to explore the marks they have left on the landscapes they once inhabited. You will notice also that he and Mary are keen disciples of the church you find best established along these coasts - and he laments when he has not bent the knee for more than a few days at a time.

Against that background it is wonderful to share his enthusiasm for the sea, the boats that sail on it, and above all for the lovely Dofesaba II - and just occasionally for his own consummate skill in arriving at tide gates at the right moment, ferry-gliding a 43-foot boat into a 44-foot berth, or a 20-metre mast under a 21 metre bridge. Real sailors can share the thrill of each of these moments - and the pleasure in the knowledge that they had happy endings.

On a cautionary note, every account Peter has penned includes an incident with the dinghy, and in this one the dinghy is upside-down, and dear Mary is in the water, and an old electric motor is destroyed and discarded, then a new one is purchased. I don't complain, stuff happens, but I fear for Mary especially for her spirit. I await the next account, in which he will miraculously find a way to keep the dinghy upright, the motor alive, and Mary on board in all serenity. Then will we acclaim Peter Bell the perfect navigator.

George Trevelyan CB
Captain of Cruising
Royal Lymington Yacht Club

Dedication

I would like to dedicate this book to all members of the Bell clan that derive from my Grandfather; William Thomas Bell (Pa) There are so many it is difficult to name them all, but especially Dominic Oliver, Francis Elliott, Stephanie Ann and Barnaby Alec Bell, without whose help we would have a boat with a boring name. Not forgetting the lovely Hollie, wife of Francis, as well as my own First (and only) Mate, the lovely Mary, without who's support none of our adventures or the writing up of them would have been possible.

Preface

This is the second book to be published featuring our adventures with our Southerly 42RST sailing yacht. The previous year we had taken Dofesaba II down the Canals du Midi to the port of Leucate where it was wintered. This book picks up in May 2019 after replacing the mast and converts our what was effectively a canal barge back into a proper sailing yacht. This book tells you about our adventures down the East coast of Spain, passing many places where British holiday makers often go for their summer holidays. I hope you will find out about some fascinating facts about parts of the areas you have "Hotelled" in, that occur just outside of the walls of your complex or even a cheap bus ride away.

I wrote these books mainly for my own purposes, but book one went down very well, and this encouraged me to continue to write the next two. You will note that what you hold in your hand is in fact two books in one,. Once I had written "The Covid year" I realised that there wasn't really enough within it to justify a separate book, so I joined it together with "The Punic Coast" . Hopefully you will agree that you have a better deal, a longer adventure to read about and a more enjoyable experience. That is definitely my intention.

Purists who read book one, will be pleased to hear that there is a lot more actual sailing in this book, and that the lifting keel (for which Southerlies are justly famous) does not factor in very much, as there aren't really many shallow harbours in the Eastern and Sothern parts of Spain, however a book about a Southerly would not be complete without at least one mention, and it does factor towards the end of 2019, where those sailors and boat owners without lifting keels will smile smugly.

Intrigued, I hope so; read on and enjoy.

Acknowledgements

My thanks to my son Dominic, as well as Siobhan and Terry, all of whom helped by crewing with us at different times. As you will read, Siobhan and Terry took a big chance and they were major contributors to several adventurous activities. My thanks to them all.

Figure 1 Plan of the first trip showing the ports & marinas visited.

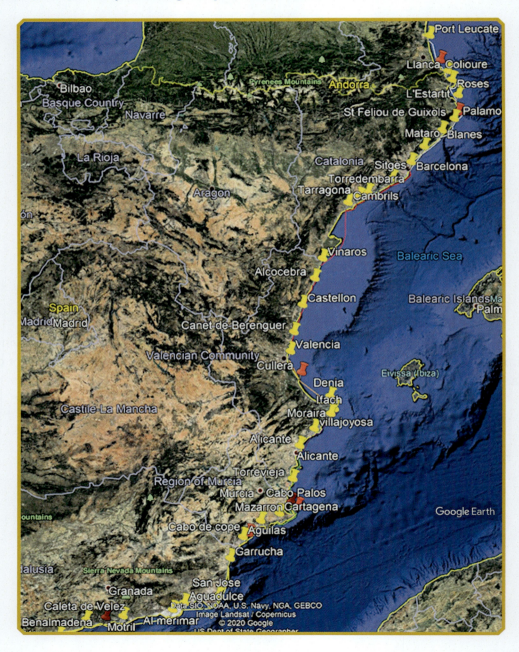

Glossary of Terms in order of appearance.

The Punic Coast – The East coast of Spain, called after the Punic wars between Roman Empire and the Carthaginian Empire 264-146 BC. The area of Spain (Hispania) that was wrestled from Carthaginian control by Rome.

Poufter Bars – An Australian expression used to describe extra handholds so that one did not miss one's step in a bouncing cockpit.

Picon – French version of Angostura bitters that can be added to a pint of Lager to give it flavour. Almost makes it taste like a pint of Bitter.

Passerelle – French for Gangplank, used by yachties as opposed to Gangplank, as that is what pirates use and we are not pirates no matter how many flags you see. Used to be a builders plank but now far more sophisticated aluminium versions exist which fold away nicely.

Force 7-8 – part of the Beaufort scale – basically very windy very bumpy and damned uncomfortable. Our boat can handle it and so can we, as we have proven several times – but it is not fun in any way. Wise skippers stay away from that.

The Mark One eyeball – basically, what you see is what you get. React only to that, no matter what the forecast says it should be. Wise advice.

Calle – Spanish for small Bay often, but not necessarily with a small sandy beach at its head. Can be a shelter if facing the right direction. Caused by a crack or fissure within the local rock and then weathered

Ria – Similar to a Calle but actually a sunken river valley often with beaches on the sides as opposed to the head – see Cornwall.

RIB – Rigid Inflatable Boat. Usually with a hard floor, with two inflatable tubes either side and a very large outboard motor on the back. Goes fast, doesn't have any sails – so a bit pointless.

Sherbets – English slang for a drink, usually alcoholic

Sun over the yardarm – a naval expression based on square rigged ships. From the quarterdeck, where the officers stood, if the angle of the sun was such that it was below the level of the yardarm – which is the large horizontal "yard" supporting the top of the mainsail, then it was late enough in the afternoon to have a drink. So time for a sherbet.

Knackered – a South London expression meaning broken. Comes from when a horse was no longer able to pull a hansom cab back in Victorian times, he was sent off to the knacker's yard for converting into glue and other rendered products.

Brighton – a seaside resort closest to London. Capital of the artistic and gay communities. Site of the first nudists beach in the UK (1979)

OTT – Over The Top; gone a bit far; way too much.

AIS – Automatic Identification System a VHF GPS Satellite based system mandatory on all ships over 300 tons. A good idea for sailing vessels which are small, unreflective and so more difficult to see on Radar Very handy.

The stand on vessel. – According to the IALA rules, the vessel that has right of way, albeit both vessels have a duty not to collide.

To T Bone another boat – to hit them in the side creating 2 right angles either side of your prow / Sharp End. If two fibre glass boats hit, the sharp end of one is flattened and it creates a hole in the side of the other. If either are made of stronger stuff (Wood/Steel/Concrete) then a more obvious disaster can occur. A manoeuvre to be avoided at all costs.

A wee taddy – a very small amount.

Marina TV – The act of watching boats manoeuvring within a Marina in the hope that the skipper is incompetent and something exciting will happen. Often well worth the wait.

A Brompton – British made folding bicycles, very light, very robust, very expensive. Popular with British cruising sailors. The wheels are only sixteen inches in diameter.

The Island – Local way of saying 'The Isle of Wight' with Yarmouth being the other end of the Lymington-Yarmouth ferry.

To Whinge – Australian slang for to Complain.

Sevriano Ballesteros – World Champion Golfer – reckoned to be the Greatest Continental European golfer of all time. He was Spanish

Singapore in 1941 – At the start of WWII the British upgraded Singapore harbour with massive 15 inch naval guns and lots of extra emplacements so as to be able to ward off any invading forces. Unfortunately no-one told the Japanese who refused to play the game properly and invaded from the North on bicycles pedalling undetected through the jungle catching the base totally by surprise.

Cabo de Gato - The Cape of the Cat. Another of these "ooooh you better be careful there" places which, if taken in reasonable weather with the correct tide and a good lookout, is not too bad. Also contains the local Spanish Coastguard base.

Crash Gybe – When sailing downwind and the boom and/or the jib swings from all the way out on one side to all the way out on the other. This can put severe stress on the rig and can be very dangerous to the sailors in the cockpit.

The Rias (of NE Spain) – a beautiful cruising ground very sheltered, with many Natural and National Parks. Lots of places for enjoying a holiday in. Ideal for lifting keel yachts like ours. Easy to get to from UK. Also known as part of Galicia.

To troll – Verb, to wander slowly yet purposefully – similar to pootle but slightly more forcefully.

Bimini – Canvas shelter on the back of the boat that connects with the sprayhood to give shelter from the sun to the whole cockpit. Allows you to drive without being burned.

To Trundle - Verb - to go forward steadily, not fast and not erratically.

The iron topsail – Sailor's slang for the engine. When clipper ships wanted to get that extra speed they let loose the topsails (Along with many others)

Mr Sulu - a Star Trek helmsman, "Full reverse thrusters" was shouted at him when the Starship Enterprise was heading into danger.

Competent Crew level – RYA sailing training has many levels of competence, of which Competent Crew is the first level.

A Decky – Sailors slang for a Deckhand, they do what the skipper says, are able to stand a watch and are part of a delivery crew. Usually young couples wanting a sailing adventure with a minute amount of cash thrown in.

Code Zero – A large sail, bigger than a genoa and smaller than a gennaker. We do not have one.

LJ – short for Life Jackets; Automatically inflating buoyancy devices designed to keep your head out of the water.

Mayday call.- a formulaic message on VHF channel 16 to let people know you are in distress and need assistance. Not to be done lightly.

Flogging – Sailor's slang for when a sail flaps rapidly back and forth. This is very annoying as it makes a nasty noise and can ruin the sail itself.

Heaving like a good'un – putting a lot of effort into it.

Farewell and fair winds – Traditional Sailor's way of saying 'Good Bye'

Slight chop. – Chop is an expression for small confused waves not coming from any one specific direction. Solent chop is well known and can cause sea sickness.

There's the rub – a Shakespearian expression (Hamlet: in the "To be or not to be" soliloquy) a rub is a flaw, as in a surface or a plan.

Boom Boom – a very British way of indicating that a joke had been told. Comes directly from a catchphrase from Basil Brush – (you will have to look that one up.)

To Pootle – Verb, to go forward whimsically. Slowly, without purpose or rush. Less than a trundle.

The Red Duster – Navy slang for the British red ensign, slightly disrespectful as all British Navy ships fly the white ensign.

To heave off – Verb; Sailor speak for to come to a stop.

Doris Stokes solution – Doris was a self professed spiritualist and professed to speak with the dead. She was known as 'The Happy Medium' This is a bit of a pun. The British like them.

South West Trains – The overground train company that serves er... the South West of the UK. Hopefully soon to be integrated back into the National British Rail.

Chapter 1
LEAVING FRANCE

The year 2018 had seen us traversing the Canals du Midi and ending up after trials and tribulations in Port Leucate. During the latter parts of April 2019, myself and Michael the official Chief Engineer of Dofesaba II had returned via ferry to Bilbao to sort out the boat and put the mast back on.

Readers of previous books will remember that on our arrival in Port Leucate (stated destination of the mast and other equipment shipped by road in September 2018) we had not been able to find ALL the equipment that had been sent there – to be precise, anything attached to the boom, or even more precise, anything that was not the mast itself, was missing. Since September 2018, Luc the yard manager had found the boom and had it transferred to his yard from the other neighbouring rival yard at a cost of £300 "for looking after it during the long cold winter". With a sigh, this extra bill was paid and we all worked together to attach mast to boat, boom to mast and generally get the vessel ready to become a sailing boat again, as opposed to a canal barge – which it wasn't.

One of the innovations I had seen on "Belfast Child" (another S42 RST) was a set of "Poufter Bars" made of Stainless Steel that the owner had had fitted to help the less steady hold onto something solid when moving around the cockpit. Michael and I had measured on B.C. the correct dimensions and had them pre-formed, so it was just a case of drilling and putting them on, and thank the Lord they fitted perfectly. We will see much later how this was a really good decision. Within four days all the work had been done, all the systems checked and the boat was back in the water. We then returned home satisfied with a job completed.

Chapter 2
ONE MONTH LATER.

So here Mary & I were, back in Port Leucate with our boat in the water, after a flight to Perpignan and taxi to the Port. Unlike September, May is cold and Port Leucate was deserted. The wind was a-whistling about the almost deserted port and only one bar was open, fortunately this was the main bar inside the harbour and they remembered us, such that a pint of Picon was poured as I entered the bar for the first time this year. Mssr & Mdme were as ever, very hospitable. It was on the way back that Mary (First Mate) found that her legs were not long enough to stretch over the mighty chasm from the concrete quay to the transom of the vessel. Having researched the fact that most marinas down the west Mediterranean coast had stern-to moorings as standard, I decided to invest in a folding gangplank (or passerelle) thereby achieving every skipper's dream of a happy crew (Very important, particularly at the start of a 5 month cruise)

Figure 2 New passerelle and a happy crew

On our last night prior to departure we invited Luc & Sophie into the cockpit for a snifter to say farewell. Dropping the line that our first port of call was in Spain, evoked much 'horreur'

"What! you are missing out Collioure – this is impossible Mssr; incorrigible. Collioure is a jewel, a masterpiece of French tourism, and good shelter from the massive storm coming up in 36 hrs time."

This last bit had me convinced, so when we took off the next day at 10.00 into 12 kts of wind from the NW, Collioure was the destination. This was a good decision, as by the time we turned into the harbour at Collioure we had two reefs in, and it was blowing twenty four knots.

When we arrived there, one could see why it was popular. The anchorage is almost totally enclosed by the arms of the bay and the water depth was "shallow" but deep enough. So we anchored well into the bay and dinghied ashore. It was now a comfortable seventeen degrees with winds greater than thirty knots but the weather just went over the top of us – which was really comforting. When we landed on the beach by dinghy, we noticed that even in May, there were plenty of tourists milling about. We could see the infrastructure was built for many more tourists than was apparent to us and so we explored the castles, windmills and the bars & restos. The next few days allowed us more time for exploration as a Force 7-8 came a-howling in from the North East which, while impressive on the outer beaches was calm with a slight rocking within the bay

Figure 3 In Collioure Bay with St Elmo's Castle and St Elmo's windmill in the back ground

Eventually we had to leave, so on a cold blustery day, we said goodbye to Collioure and headed out into a cold North-Westerly, but as usual the weather forecast steered us poorly and the wind died within the hour to - none at all. So on with Iron Topsail (as they say on the big sailing ships) until we hit the coast at Llanca. (metaphorically speaking). We were now in Spain.

A DIVERSION ON WEATHER FORECASTS –

A good skipper tries hard to obtain viable and meaningful weather forecasts. This is best done with the mark one eyeball, giving you thirty minutes warning, but these days we all want to KNOW what will happen for the rest of the voyage, or at least the next five days. On the East coast of Spain, I decided to look at the BBC weather app, Predict Wind and Yacht Weather, then make a judgement based on the results. As these three seem to get their raw data from similar sources, you will not be surprised to hear that in the main, they agreed with each other.

Unfortunately in a measured 90% of the time, they forgot to inform the wind gods, Hanui-o-rangi and Hine-tu-whenua included. We spent 5 months diligently looking up the weather and laughing later, when once again it turned out to be completely wrong. Rule one of East Spain cruising, only the Mk 1 eyeball works and you only get thirty minutes warning.

Chapter 3
ARRIVING IN CATALONIA.

Figure 4 Golden Crucifix with Emeralds, Rubies and crushed diamonds in the shawl

From Llanca it was a chance to explore the hinterland. We decided to visit Figueres from here. The bus was regular, clean and very cheap. (as all are in this part of Spain – eg Catalunya) We joined the four other Brits on the bus and got off in the main square. The main attraction of Figueres is the Salvador Dali museum. When I say THE Salvador Dali museum, I really mean one of the many Salvador Dali museums, as he was a very wealthy chap and had a clear vision of his own genius, and he knew that in future times everyone would like to know more about him. Was he a great artist? I am not qualified to answer that, all I can tell you is that as a young man he was a very good artist in the more conventional sense where paintings are concerned and he was a genius where it came to beautiful jewelled objects. His ability to shock & confuse came in his later years and when you're surrounded by so much confused art work it makes you doubt your own sanity. However it is very wonderful, and a never-to-be-missed experience, and I could have stayed there all day but by 14:00 hrs my beer tank was empty and Mary needed some sustenance. We returned to the boat and prepared for leaving the following day.

The following day dawned with blue skies and fluffy white clouds, the winds were light and variable, it seemed very pleasant. This part of the Costa Brava is very rugged with many Calles. (A calle is an inlet or sometimes a ria) If the weather is good and you are prepared, these mini-rias are sheltered and lovely to sit in with a picnic and as we passed them, we did see some motor cruisers doing exactly that, but we had to arrive at our next destination in time to obtain a berth, and the wind was picking up. There was an intriguing "inside passage" around the headland which looked exciting/challenging, however as it was getting a bit bumpy, I was insufficiently able to convince the crew of this great idea for a minor adventure/digression and so around the safe outside way we went.

Figure 5 Map of internal passage.

And so we get to Roses. It is blowing, rain is in the air and we are still in May. (24th actually). We parked the boat and started to explore. Easier said than done, we had seventeen knots on the beam as we tried to fit into a very tight berth, we also had two incompetent rope catchers on the Quay. After three attempts with no proper communication going on, the local "old boy" arrived, got into a rib and added some assistance by barking in Catalan at the two incompetents, as well as a helpful nudge with his prow, as gusts made life tricky. Obviously, we got in with a little gel coat clunk at the back due to further incompetence and soon we were all tied up and safe, but it did take thirty minutes.

Roses has been a port since Punic times (300 BC) but today the whole area is covered by a 17th cent Vauban fort, known locally as the Citta Della. It was one of the ports that supplied troops and naval vessels to the Armada and also used to receive Silver, Gold and other treasures from the New World.

During the excavations in the '60s & '70s archaeologists found evidence of Roman occupation within the fort area and started to explore. As they dug down past the Roman remains there were signs of an earlier Greek settlement set out on a completely different axis. Recent work has shown that the Greeks built on and over even earlier settlements, contemporary with the early Iberians and there was also evidence of the traders who plied the Mediterranean and further afield. We call them the Phoenicians from the Greek for the people who lived in the Levant or what we now call Lebanon & Israel. We do not know what they called themselves as they did not feel the need to say "er.. We are Phoenicians" as they didn't speak Greek. They were more likely to be descendants of previous empires, Babylonian or even Persian.

During our exploration down this coast we came across this sequence of occupation so often (with some extra nuances) that this narrative may sometimes seem repetitive, but looking at the coast and the way the winds work and vary with the seasons, one can deduce that it is an easy place to trade with, if coming from the East in the winter and returning to the East in the Autumn. Also, this area has always been very productive agriculturally over at least 3 millennia that no wonder everyone wanted a piece of the action.

Here in Roses we were able to see the evidence before us on a cold blustery day in May.

Figure 6 Roman walls on top of Greek walls within the Citta Della of Roses

The following day we took a bus to the Roman city and port of Empurias. I was advised to do this by my Catalonian friend, Luis Herrera, who as a child had played in the sand that then covered the site. He remembers when there were no boundaries and people could come in and picnic amongst the stones and wonder who had put them there. In his time there was no Archaeological site, just stones and sand. He did not realise he was playing on top of one of Spain's major 1st century Roman cities.

We just had to go there to see this once thriving city, abandoned in the 15th Cent and covered with sand until recently. It is enormous with clear distinction between Iberian, Greek, Carthaginian (Punic) Republican Roman, Imperial Roman, Visigoths, Vikings, then the Moors, the Christian kings & eventually the Catalan Dukes. Whereupon in the 17th Century it died as a town, probably due to the port silting up and an inland town becoming more prosperous (it happens).

I loved Empurias, there was so much to see and so much untouched ROMAN, you could feel the hand of the Emperor Augustus on your back. We went through both Old Empurias (mainly Greek) and New Empurias (mostly Roman) and the museum, so we were very tired at the end of the day. It was now getting positively warm and definitely time for a beer back in the Marina.

Figure 7 One of many astounding original mosaics

A SMALL HISTORICAL ASIDE –

We in our Island kingdom way north of the Mediterranean Sea often forget that war has been waged for over 3000 yrs within Europe as we know it. Mostly over "territory", which included agricultural land, but also mines containing metals, and sometimes, just sheer territory for the fun of it. The East coast of Spain is "cursed" by having many areas of flat fertile agricultural land (even now) as well as mountains containing Gold, Silver, Lead, Iron, Zinc and other important and necessary-for-development type minerals, such that to hold on to these resources requires a bigger army and better defences than your neighbour. The fighting on this coast has been persistent and unstoppable since pre-Carthaginian times (the Carthaginian descendants of the Ancient Greeks nicked it from the local iron age tribes we call the Iberians) and the remains of their cities and defences remain as evidence, ready to be exploited and revealed by archaeologists of the 21st Century. The only peoples we know of that did not fight in this area are the Ancient Egyptians and the Phoenicians who preferred to trade and go back home instead of fighting and staying.

Chapter 4
Towards the bigger towns

Within a day or two we had exhausted Roses and it was time to move on to Lestartit. Fortunately the sun came out and a good sail with the wind on our port quarter took us there very swiftly. This town has little to recommend it, except a fine marina and a Castle on top of a hill. Everyone loves a castle, well I do, however Mary the crew, was not a fan. To get there was a cheap bus ride away, then a very healthy climb uphill to the Castell de Montgris.

Figure 8 The Montgris Castle - from the bottom

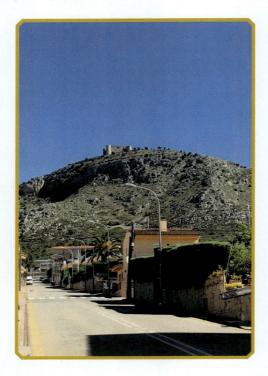

This was a fascinating place as it was built in 13th-14th cent as a direct copy of a Crusader castle, mainly because the knight who built it, had only ever seen castles when he was off in the crusades and thought that was the way to do it. As can be seen from the photographs, this design was completely inappropriate for the VERY steep terrain and distance from the coast and local town, which is what the castle was trying to defend. After building the outer walls, the inside was left uncompleted, and it was left to rot to pieces and never saw "action".

Having climbed the hill, I would not have liked to be the donkey or the peasant humping blocks of stone up to it. To ease my aching knees, I returned to the boat for a soothing beer and to tell Mary of my exciting climb. We decided to leave early as a forty five knot breeze was expected later on in the day.

We intended to anchor in a Calle or even use a buoy, if it was available. We had read about a really good cove with Restos and many facilities just down the coast in a place called Tamariu and it was sheltered from the expected winds. We arrived and Mary caught the buoy first time, which pleased her greatly (and me). We were just settling down for a sandwich and a nice cup of tea when there was banging on the hull. An English voice explained that "You can't park that boat here mate, you'se too big, that buoy has a maximum length of 32 foot".

Well this was a blow, but being British we moved further out to the bigger buoys (as in "hanging around with the Bigger Boys") We were not quite so successful with buoy catching this time, but after lots of effort we were tied up and safe. Just at that moment with my boat hook still in hand, out came a very fast angry RIB.

"This Calle and all the Buoys, which I own are now closed – you must leave, you have five minutes"

Well that was not very friendly, I decided against causing a diplomatic incident by bopping him on the bonce with my trusty boathook, sighed; and prepared the boat and crew for departure. Such is character built.

After that we tried to get into the next small port of Llanfranc but we were again turned away as there was no room, so it was ever onward.

On the 29th May we came to Palamos. This town has a double harbour either side of a large lump of rock. The theory being that depending on the wind, one can shelter in an anchorage or a Marina either side.

Figure 9 All is nice and gentle as we land on the beach

As the winds were expected forty five knots we stayed in the Eastern Marina for one night, but as the price, even the cheap rate was of €77.0 per noce, we decided to leave the next day. As we had not "anchored" for a day or two, well since Collioure in fact (see several pages north of here) and seeing as how the wind was nice and gentle and coming from the NE, we decided to anchor in the Bay South West of the large lump of rock. What could be more sheltered and safe. Down went the anchor – setting perfectly first time. Out came the electric outboard engine, down from the push pit went the un-electric dinghy and after connecting the two and putting the full crew with associated paraphernalia into said pneumatic vessel, off we went to the shore. All went very well, the beach was deserted and a beach café was open and welcoming. So welcoming in fact that we stayed there for lunch and a few sherbets. Eventually the sun went over the yardarm and it was time to return to the Dofesaba II and prepare for dinner. Back we went to the dinghy lying gently on the sand. I reconnected the battery which I carried in my rucksack for security. I then looked up and noticed that while we had been relaxing, the waves had increased in size and a healthy swell was now crashing happily onto the beach.

When we had landed, the wind was in the NE and the waves lapped gently onto the slightly sloping beach. Now the wind was in the SW and the waves were a good 40 cm high. Not a problem for a 42 ft Southerly RST but for a dinghy whose freeboard is 0.3m it is a bit near to the knuckle. By the time I had moved the dinghy out of the new extended surf zone, I was waist deep in water. Just as I pushed down on the side of the dinghy to get myself in, a wave hit us, Mary stumbled on a small shelf under the water, the dinghy turned sideways to the surf and said dinghy overturned on top of my head.

Well I was very pleased that the maintenance I had done on my lifejacket was adequate, as with a big pop my life jacket inflated and I was in the water under an upside down dinghy. This was not good. Getting to my feet in 1/2m of water, I was able to shrug off the dinghy and right it. All our stuff was scattered about in the water, so we set to recovering it all, including the two paddles I always put in. I tried the electric motor, but surprise surprise, it was as dead as a doornail which was not too unexpected given the circumstances. However we still had to re-launch the dinghy into the ever increasing surf and get to the boat. You will be pleased to hear that we did accomplish this, not without some exhortation to the Crew to paddle harder, as otherwise we would go round in circles and back to the beach.

Arriving at the transom VERY warm and salty, we re-embarqued and got sorted out. The electric engine was totally knackered and now useless, no matter how much I tried to dry it out. We settled down to a nice dinner and a pleasant evening, convinced we had survived another incident. As you can imagine there are no photos of this, as we were too busy, but hopefully I have painted a sufficient picture with the last thousand words.

Chapter 5
CRUISING WITHOUT A POWERED DINGHY TO BARCELONA

As May came to a close the following day, we travelled to St Feliu de Grixolles, with a small sail in twelve knots of wind while the sky stayed blue. This is a charming port town that had the distinction of being the "end of the line" of one of the first public railways in Spain, now discontinued. Quite unusual to see steam locomotives within the local cafes and bars – but it happens here. There is as ever, a lovely beach and pleasant architecture and a nice marina. Apparently it really comes alive in August. We couldn't hang around that long.

The next day we left for Blanes in light winds and blue skies – this was turning more into a holiday. Now it was June which meant more people and higher Marina fees. Blanes is the gateway to the Costa Brava, but only if coming from the South, which to be fair is what most people do. The intrepid crew of Dofesaba II rarely, if ever, do things that most people do. I suppose we just like to be adventurous in many things.

A very small aside – The Costa Brava translates as the "rough" coast – in that you have to be brave to go along it. Well maybe that is true in the winter but apart from a few strong winds, we did not suffer. There are many Calles (Coves, Rias, sheltered anchorages if you like) most often with a sandy beach at the end of it and steep rocky sides. Apart from them there are also some lovely little old Roman ports, which until the last century could only be visited by boat.

Blanes itself has little to recommend it being a small holiday village on the edge of Lloretta del Mar which is a lot more commercialised.

The following day was slightly windy with blue skies. We tried several times to sail pleasantly, but when the boat speed drops below two knots it is engine-on time and so we eventually got to Port Mataro. This is another small port/marina to the north of Barcelona. We walked around the town but there was nothing special about it.

Figure 10 Mary outside the RCNB

Then it was on to Barcelona the next day. A fresh breeze of Force four to five and seventeen degrees C. all helped to make the four hour journey very relaxing. Barcelona was the only place I had pre-booked before we set off from England. I had looked up the Real Club Nautico Barcelona and this appeared to be a very well set up "Royal" yacht club. Established in 1896 it was even older than many in the UK including the RLymYC. I had even booked a berth there. When we arrived, our pilot book was a little out of date and I could not find the entrance to the RCNB, but there was a brand new walkway stopping all vessels entering. I looked carefully, there must be an entrance as there were lots of masts on the other side of the walkway – I just couldn't find it at all. I called on the VHF and eventually saw pedestrians being stopped and then the whole walkway slid open revealing an entrance. Feeling a bit silly that I might be going into the wrong one (which to be fair one can always sort out "later" once you are safe) I nosed in and turned right, as it turned out, to the Yacht Club Barcelona. Then into view came a helpful Spaniard, pointing the other way, to the RCNB which was indicated on a tiny little notice that I had missed. As there wasn't room to turn, it was full reverse thrusters and I reversed 500m to my correct berth, receiving several quizzical glances from sailors on their boats, as in "what is that stupid Englishman doing that for". The RCNB were very pleased to see us as there had been no other visitors so far this season. We enjoyed their huge bar and Restaurant all by ourselves. When we arrived and showed our RLymYC membership cards we were greeted rather effusively by the Bar Steward (He was a very nice man really) Well we thought 'this is nice, to be so welcomed and we are complete strangers'. It turns out that during our wanderings the RLymYC had been accepted into the International Association of Royal Yacht Clubs June 2018 and we were their first visitors with a boat. I suppose they were on their best behaviour because they could not do enough for us.

Here we were joined by our first son Dominic (the D.O. in Dofesaba as he introduces himself within the sailing community) and spent five days enjoying the sites of Barcelona. The Sagrida Familia cathedral had been finished a lot more since we were last here in 2004, and this time we had a chance to visit the Picasso

Figure 11 La Duena by Picasso

and the Joan Miro museums. I did not realise that Picasso was so good. Some of his stuff from the age of 16-25 is remarkable and very beautiful, I have to admit that a Picasso squiggle on a blank piece of canvas does not do very much for me no matter what shade of blue it is.

The Miro exhibition was as expected, very two dimensional and very simplistic. Some was clever and some just pointless, but it had to be visited.

In Barcelona I was able to buy the new upgraded (and fully waterproof) Torqueedo T1001 Electric motor for the Dinghy. We had missed out on many lovely Calles to anchor in, as we did not have propulsion, well now we did. We were back to being proper cruisers again.

After five days, it was time for Dom to return to work and us to leave for Sitges, our next port of call.

Figure 12 Both side aisles of the Sagrida Familia. Stained Glass infused with natural sun light

Figure 13 Port Leucate to Barcelona

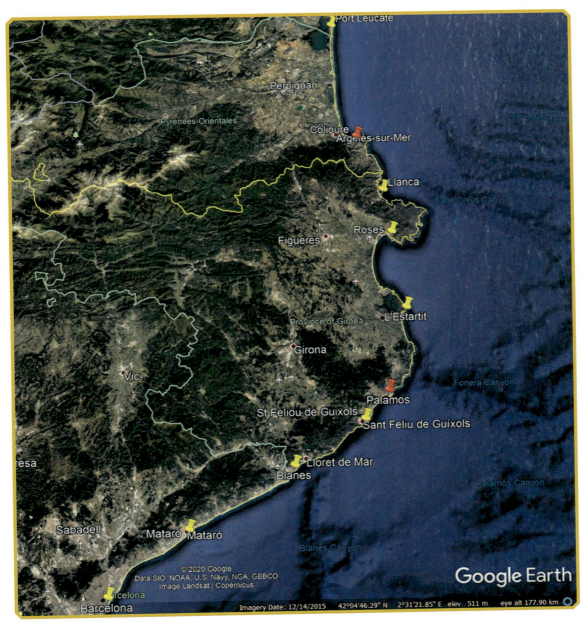

Chapter 6
OFF TO TARRAGONA

❧

We left the RCNB at 09:30 hrs sailing through the walkway then out into the main harbour. The wind was just fine and all sails were up as we turned the corner to leave the main harbour and just managed to avoid a supertanker leaving the oil port on the other side of the wall (we had both been sailing along, completely invisible to each other. I doubt if he saw me, so I wisely let him go first and went around his stern) The rules of the sea are all fine and dandy but some times a little common sense and courtesy goes a long way to staying safe.

Figure 14   A puzzled looking statue early 20th Cent. by the nudist beach.

We had a nice sail to Sitges and arrived at the anchorage well sheltered from the North Easterly wind by the breakwater. We dropped the hook and it bit first time – but after thirty minutes we realised that without any wind the boat had a propensity to turn side on to the South Westerly swell and we rocked in an alarming manner. I very nicely up-anchored, and moved closer to the breakwater for a bit more shelter and tried again. Same result, very annoying. After several more tries we decided that we would have to "Marina" after all. I was a bit disappointed but what can you do.

Sitges is the LBGBTXQ capital of Spain, a bit like Brighton but with more sand and sea. It has 3-4 nudist beaches one of which is designated a "Homosexual beach", the others are not, which I suppose was Spain's way of allowing this part of the community to have their own space where they could feel comfortable. It must work as it was relatively crowded, whereas the other beaches were less so. There were also several beaches that were designated "Family" beaches, which was a tad confusing as if you were a homosexual couple with several children, where do you go ? Oh well I suspect the local folk had got it all sorted, and as we were only there for a day or two I refused to worry about it. As we strolled about, we saw some amazing sights. Coming out of a bar I was almost run down by a young man on six inch platform boots that went up to his thighs. Above that was a silvery leather G String, leaving very little to the imagination, then topped with a peacock feathered waistcoat and heavy make up and back brushed hair. He certainly made an impression. He was not alone either, as we strolled along the promenade with an independent air, we saw several young gentlemen of similar OTT persuasion. Very different. I think the Spanish society have come a very long way since the end of the Franco regime, particularly in Sitges.

Soon it was time to leave for Tarragona, another city I looked forward to visiting. Traditionally it is where Altar-wine comes from, and I was looking forward to trying it out to see if it would bring back memories of my childhood, as I had been an altar boy in Catholic churches since the age of four until sixteen and would often sneak a sip of the wine used for Communion as any inquisitive boy would do. (and they nearly all did)

Figure 15 Free Catalonia; we'll sing if you don't

We left Sitges in a force four to five with fluffy clouds and a temperature of below twenty degrees all day, so quite pleasant in a way. But I see from the log that there was a lot of swell making it a little bumpy. After six hours we came into Tarragona Port Esportiu and moored up stern-to really nicely. Tarragona is a very historic city and the following morning we decided to get up early and explore. Unfortunately it was pouring with rain. We wandered into the main city by bus and when we got off, we found ourselves within a "Free Catalonia" demonstration. There were about 100 people huddled under umbrellas all about our own age (around 55-75) listening to a man standing on a real soapbox. He was; as they all do, speaking rapidly in Spanish or Catalonian (we being English struggle to tell the difference) using one arm to punctuate the sentences. At that moment he jumped down and started singing what I could only assume was the Catalonian National Anthem, using said arm as a baton to encourage the other 99. There was a ragged yet damp response for several verses, then they all packed up and dispersed for a coffee. I felt this was quite a remarkable event in that there were also two squad cars with four armed police standing by chatting happily to themselves. The rest of Tarragona carried on around this group, some smiling, some nodding in agreement and a few even joining in with the verses, yet most just ignored them and carried on with their daily lives. A bit like being in London really.

Figure 16 The Roman amphitheatre Tarragona

Figure 17 Human tower

We then went on to see the Roman amphitheatre and part of the Circus Maximus, which has been uncovered and displayed over the last ten years, followed by a visit to the main Basilica and associated quadrangle and cloisters, which were once again the "best in Spain" . This was followed by the Forum and remains of the old city and then a walk along the old Roman Wall (originally, quite low, but then built up over the years until "finished off" by Carlos IV) which had lots of Roman statues on it that the archaeologists had found dotted about the gardens. We also came across a bronze statue of the village human tower building so favoured in this part of the world. It is a particularly Catalonian thing where each village tries to get a small child higher than any other village. We had seen this in Beziers (France) with real people, but here was a lifesize statue showing how it was done.

After several days we had "done" Tarragona and it was time to move on to go and meet our friends, Jeff Proudfoot and his wife Sharon. We had tried to book a berth in Peniscola where Jeff lived, but had not received any reply. So we asked Jeff to pop down and do a recce. His report was not ideal.

"The Harbour Master has been retired and they haven't appointed a new one yet"

"Ah that's a bit of a blow – well we can slip in then, no-one will notice"

"Oh and by the way – there isn't any room there"

"Ah! that's going to be a bit tricky then."

A new plan was formulated for us to stop at Vinaros, so off we went. It was a beautiful day. The sky was blue and a fifteen knot wind was on the beam, the swell was a bit awkward but apart from that it was lovely. We sailed along happily.

Autopilot on, sails all set, constant breeze, all I had to do was to keep a look out. I was daydreaming away, when something on the horizon ahead of us, just forward of the Port beam caught my eye. The object looked like a fishing boat, but it was a bit too wide. This soon resolved into two fishing boats. I went to the chartplotter to see if it was on AIS and to check the CPA or closest point of approach. Well not only was the first fishing boat doing twenty knots and the CPA was only ten metres but so were the other 9, and as it turned out, these were just the ones with AIS on, there were another five without AIS. It transpired that I was heading at six knots into a fishing fleet doing their best to get home with their catch as fast as they could go and I was er... to put it bluntly, right in the way.

Figure 18 Chartplotter image showing Spanish fishing fleet

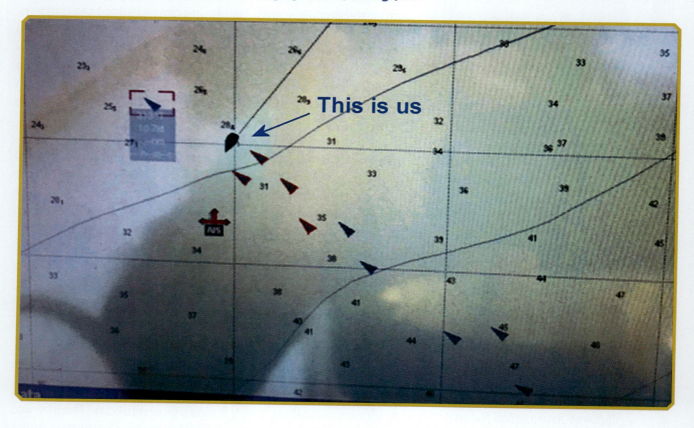

I suggested Mary come on deck to help keep an eye out, while I thought about it. Several factors zipped through my brain

1) I was a sailing vessel and they were definitely not sailing, so I had priority, but did those fishermen KNOW that.
2) While I was on a port tack I was showing them my port light and I could see their starboard lights, which also gave me an element of priority.

I decided the best thing was to act like the stand on vessel (which I was) and hold my speed and course, however, I also put the engine on and left it in neutral ready for any necessary rapid course change. Mary and I then held our breath as they thundered towards us. Approximately half a mile from us, the lead boat, which had been heading for a T Bone, delicately switched a degree to port and boat number two also destined to come rather close, twitched a wee taddy to starboard. As they creamed past us both crews came out of their wheel houses and waved in a very friendly manner, the rest of the fleet passed either side of us – all waving happily, still at twenty knots. We breathed a sigh of relief and continued our otherwise uneventful journey to Vinaros. And when we get there, who was waiting on the quay – but Jeff, who then took us to his place. Our first opportunity to be on land in a house and to interact with other humans not including ourselves for quite a while.

Chapter 7
PENISCOLA AND WESTWARDS

We thoroughly enjoyed being on land for a few days and we explored Peniscola (careful with that pronunciation) which is the site of the habitation of Benedict XIII the last of the Aragonese popes. He lived here in a massive Templar castle under siege for four and a half years and was a well loved and very Christian pope, unlike many of his predecessors and antecedents, particularly those originally named Borgia. When he died, the line of Aragonese popes died with him and the papacy returned to Rome under one of the Borgias. The castle is a massive and imposing structure unused since the 15th Cent. And well worth a look. Apparently it is used within the Game of Thrones series.

Figure 19 Statue of the popular pope Benedict XII outside the Templar Castle walls

During the next five days we lounged, and on our last but one day took Jeff and Sandra for a trip around the bay. It wasn't very bumpy or of long duration, but Sandra did not enjoy it, so we returned to port for our last dinner together before carrying on our merry way.

Figure 20 Peniscola Templar built Castle

After a meal that night complete with genuine Flamenco Dancers and strummy guitars we said goodbye to Jeff & Sandra and prepared for the next day's trip to Alcossebra, which was a lovely little port just down the road (OK Two hrs) from Peniscola. This town is so small there is little really to see. BUT on one of the beaches is a rare geological phenomenon. The beach leaks.

I had better explain. The hills to the rear of Alcossebre, the Sierra D'Irta are made of Limestone as is much of southern Spain. This limestone over the Millenia, has been washed away by the constant movement of water causing underground rivers and canyons. The water follows the force of gravity until it hits an impervious layer (for instance a layer of mudstone or Clay/Shale) whereupon the water has to go sideways. On this beach, known as the Playa Las Fuentes (Beach of the Springs) the layer of mudstone is topped by sand. So freezing cold fresh mountain water leaks out of the beach and into the sea. Many of the Spaniards build little mini dams so as to make a pool so that in the heat of the day they can refresh themselves with cool water. I tried this, but it was about four degrees C so, not to my liking, as I prefer the upper 20's. The sea was also "not hot" being about fifteen degrees. This did not stop many hundreds of Spaniards enjoying being on the beach beside the sea.

The next day turned out nice again (Muther) and a gentle breeze (eight to twelve knots) came from our port quarter. We didn't have far to go to Castellon de la Plana so it was time to try the Gennaker. We have not had a lot of success with this sail even after I have had the furling mechanism modified. Anyway it came out beautifully and flew like a Gennaker should for all of about two minutes, whereupon the wind went from ENE to ESE, not a gross change you might suggest, but enough to put us off course or cause the Gennaker to flap. We spent an hour trying to get the dang thang working properly and just as we did, yes you guessed it the wind changed to a Southerly aspect. By now I was getting fed up, as the Gennaker is supposed to help us sail more swiftly "downwind". A southerly wind was just off the nose so in came the sail and on went the engine. We pulled into Castellon after trying them on the VHF and the phone to no avail, so we just pulled in and found a berth that fitted. We had to wait until 1700 for the Office to open to confirm we could stay the night. (To be fair there was no way we were leaving no matter what they said). We visited the Real Club Nautico but they would not let us use their facilities as we were not members. This being in direct contravention of what was written in our pilot book. Strangely, this happened all the time in Spain. The pilot book suggested we would be more than welcome in the local Club Nautico, particularly for a dip in the pool when it got hotter, however the Club owners had not read our pilot book and while we were allowed to use the bar & food (as was any Tom, Dick or Manuel) we were not allowed inside the pool area even tho' we had paid our mooring fees. I thought this was a big swizz, but there was little I could do about it. I tried stamping my foot and expleting loudly, but it made no difference. (Must explain this to American actors).

So after a refreshing shower in the PORT facilities (nowhere near as good) it was bed time so as to be ready for the next day.

In this point of the narrative it is now the 20th June and we are going South and West, generally aiming for Canet de Berenguer. Just after we left Castellon I happened to glance down at the chart plotter and saw the Easting or Latitude go from 00.00.01E to 00.00.01W in a matter of seconds. We had just gone over the Meridian. I felt a sense of accomplishment as that had not happened since last year on the 2nd of July when we had passed through a tiny hamlet called Hure within a few miles of the start of the Canal de Garonne on our adventure through the Canals du Midi. I remember it well, as it was my 64th Birthday, and I spent all morning trying to fix a blocked engine inlet pipe. Ahhh! of such small events are sweet memories made.

Chapter 8
CANET DE BERENGUER & VALENCIA

This journey was a lovely little sail of five hours with the Force four wind behind my left shoulder, just ideal for a Southerly, so when it came time to berth stern to, I came down the channel between the pontoons (slowly) swung the bows over with the rudder and a bit of bow thruster and put the gears into reverse. We did not slow down. Ran the engine to full revs, lots of water being thrust out the sides but no decrease in speed. I was probably doing one knot but definitely aiming towards a small Merry Fisher. (which is a small personal fishing boat) I could feel the panic behind my eyes while I desperately came out of gear and back into reverse again, at last I could feel the bite, BUT our bowsprit was perilously close to the windows of the Merry Fisher, using the bow thruster again I saved us a few inches and with a little "dink" we connected. The pranged vessel gave a tiny little rock as Dofesaba II gently went backwards towards her berth. None of this was missed by the usual crowd of Marina TV watchers, including several fishermen and two Marineros who very nicely helped me berth. By that time I was shaking from the adrenalin high. I explained in my best franco-anglo-spanish that the feathering prop must have got stuck in neutral and so I did not have full control, and that I would of course pay for any damage to the aforesaid Merry Fisher.

Figure 21 The dink on the molested vessel

The Dink

This kept every one happy, so after ensuring our vessel was all safe and sound, I went with my papers to examine the Merry Fisher and to take photos of any possible damage and then to proceed to the Capitania.

With some trouble I got onto the Merry Fisher and tried hard to find any damage, because er... there wasn't any. Looks like I had just pushed a solid part of the wheelhouse with the bowsprit. ('tis true that the Lord shines upon the righteous). I told the office that there had been no damage.

Several hours later we saw a local person clamber onto the Merry Fisher accompanied by what could be taken as an engineer, they peered and poked and looked and examined, but I heard no more about it. I was very fortunate.

The following day I went down underwater and looked at the prop, no it was not too cold, but pretty dirty, and there was nothing to see. I can only assume the feathering prop had got a bit stuck with some sea critter or bit of weed within the mechanism, but now this had all been cleared. I resolved there and then to try a burst of reverse WELL before I ever needed it as I approached any berth, and this I did for the rest of the trip.

The next day I cycled up the wadi (or dry stream bed) to view the old Roman settlement of Segundum, which I thoroughly enjoyed. What was not so good was the advertised cycle track there and back. When you only have little wheels on a Brompton, big stones and tree roots get a bit bumpy, also there was not a graded signed path as we have here in the New Forest, just indicators to suggest a path through the debris.

A SMALL DIVERSION ON DRY STREAM BEDS

These dry stream beds (in Arabic we would call them Wadis) are full of detritus from the mountains that nearly always lie behind the coastal plain, as is right and proper and occurs in most countries except ours. (UK). The detritus can in some cases be house-sized boulders but that is rare, most of the boulders tend to max out at about half a metre, but even that coming down with the full force of the water from a winter storm in the mountains can wreck a person, let alone a house. It was good to see the Spanish NOT building where there was evidence of the full force of flood water, unlike the Middle East and to some extent the UK. (In regard to floodplains)

I returned to the boat a bit sore and with my historical exploration tank fully topped up, whereupon Mary had found out that tomorrow was the feast of St Joan, and there was going to be a FIESTA. "Huzzah" we cried as we had always managed to miss these wherever we went.

"Oooooh you should have been here last week for the Fiesta, it was wonderful" we have often heard.

"Well unfortunately we were battling the elements 'out there'" is my reply.

"Yes but next year you really have to see the Bulls running/Parade of Statues/Lobster tickling/Flower Floats" etc. delete as appropriate. So for us this was quite nice and we resolved to join in as much as we could.

Figure 22 Brazilian Salsa band - Spanish style

Come the evening we followed a Brazilian salsa band (No they were not all hairless), who were a pleasant diversion with many young people beating their drums. We were semi-pleased to see they were not as good as the "more mature" version we see every year at the Yarmouth Festival on the Island, who are excellent, but seeing them, and listening to their drumming raised the spirits.

We also attended the Sardine Eating Festival – whereupon our tickets were asked for and not produced, as we did not know we had to get them from a cubicle a half a km away and a half an hour ago. However, a very nice Frenchman seeing our plight, used his spare tickets to get us some. Then, as it was now dark, it was onto the beach to see all the families around their fire pits burning lots of driftwood which they had hauled down to the beach from their personal stores. In fact, all day we had seen fit young men with wheel barrows transporting odd bits of wood from the boots of Seats onto the beach, making several trips. It is said that if you go into the sea on the feast of St Joan and jump over three waves you will be blessed with a boy child. I have to admit that it was a bit more complicated than that when Mary and I had our three boys, but it was a good excuse for a fiesta anyway. By now, most fires were down to embers, and then the fireworks started. To be nice, each firework was well appreciated for several minutes before the next was sent up. This was a little protracted for us, so we toddled off to our boat for to sleep.

Figure 23 The Holy Grail - How many books on sailing include a picture of THAT

Come the post dawn, we were off to Valencia, capital city of the province. Again another lovely day's sail without drama. Pulled in, went to the bar, nice lazy day. Cleaned the log, bought a new starter battery, usual stuff. Valencia marina itself is enormous, but really lovely. It is a really long walk from ANY berth to the bus stop, let alone the town centre. The area is filled with bars and clubs (none of which would let us in, except for lunch or "Just a Drink") spread out along what was obviously the old docks. Now the area has set itself up for superyachts and cruise ships. I was pleased to see that this area was supplemented by the use of electric scooters on which I had a go. However when I read how many Euros I had needed to get from one end to the other I decided that my aged legs could manage it. We stayed four days in this wonderful old city visiting the Oceanarium, the Basilica, with its Genuine "Holy Grail" chapel and several Irish bars, that seemed to be popular down this coast. In most cases we used the Bus network, that I felt worked very well, particularly for us, as the Marina was a fair way from the centre.

Figure 24 Barcelona to Valencia

Chapter 9
VALENCIA TO ALICANTE

Eventually we had to leave Valencia and try a day out at anchor. The opportunity presented itself here as the next marina was just that tiny bit too far away for a leisurely hop and there was a very nice cape with good shelter from the wind and swell, so we tried it. Full sails up with the engine ticking over we cruised at five knots in an eight knot wind. We got to the bay, dropped anchor and it bit first time. Out with the Dinghy onto the beach. Our first real try-out of the new electric engine, which worked perfectly, as expected. Mary stayed on the beach while Peter went off to find a mini-mart to get some essential supplies. After two hours of fruitless marching, I had established that we had parked on the beach of a holiday development that had forgotten to put all-day bars and mini marts into the plan. Fully disgruntled I returned to the beach café. Whereupon I whinged at the proprietor that there weren't any mini-marts about.

"What would you like Senor"

"Well some bread, milk, beer & wine as we are running low"

"No problem Senor we can give you all of those" and he said this with a welcoming Spanish smile.

Figure 25 Parked in the shallows near Cabo Cullera

What a lovely surprise. How jolly nice, apart from the fact I had wasted two hours in the hot sun only to find that what I needed was on my doorstep, but I put that down to my own stupidity. I probably paid a little extra, but why not, as HE had gone to the trouble of getting the provisions in.

We bundled back into the Dinghy and spent a fine night on board. Ready to leave in the morning.

The following morning it was off to Denia in no wind. Anchor came up well, engine on, away we go, mainsail out, revs set to 2000. Mary returns to snooze mode and all proceeds well. As the day went on, the wind starts to increase. At eight knots the jib comes out and the engine goes off and we sail all the way to Denia. As we arrive we have to take the sails in with twenty three knots over the deck, which is not so easy but we did it, as ever. Into the marina, and fortunately the wind dies to about twelve knots which can still be tricky. Soon we're nicely tied up and ready for a beer.

A SMALL ASIDE REGARDING THE ISLAS BALIERAS

Denia is the set off point for vessels wishing to explore the Islas Balieras, which is something I had been contemplating for some time. While we had been in Valencia we had met several people that had just come from there and said how crowded all the anchorages were and how impossible it was to get a berth in the marinas. It was by now the beginning of July so we were into high season where marina prices are hiked to the n'th degree. (Market Forces deah boy) and while I do not mind paying €50/noce, North of €150/noce is not my idea of enjoyment. We had also heard tales of very bad weather close to these islands which had damaged at least two of the yachts that had ended up in Valencia. So after discussions and thoughts, we decided to miss the Balearics out of our journey.

It turns out that if we had left when we had planned to, we would have been caught in a very nasty storm half way across. We found out that this had fried the instruments of the yacht we spoke to later in Cartagena, who was there having himself repaired. Apparently several yachts limped into San Antonio (Main Marina/port of Ibiza) badly frightened and damaged over the next day or two. Several having been struck by lightning. As happens a few times, I was happy with my decision.

Otherwise Denia was quite boring, apart from spending my 65th birthday in a very nice restaurant there and watching the Lionesses (England's Women's National Football team) lose, it was uneventful, so we left for Moreira the next day.

The journey took us past some incredible rock formations totally prohibiting any landing, but they looked lovely in the sunshine.

Figure 26 Some very nice Limestone - note the lighthouse

Strangely enough Moreira was also very boring with nothing to say for it at all, so the following day we left for Calpe.

Calpe is another of these well sheltered bays, particularly from the North and East, where most of our wind was coming from. The shelter is formed by a massive limestone rock called the Penon of Ilfach, which towers over the marina. It looked fascinating.

"The guidebook says there is a track up to the top, accessible to all walkers"

"Well let's do it then" Says I

"Not on your Nelly am I going up there in thirty degrees" says the lovely Mary, and so it was that half an hour later with sandals on my feet and a small juice in my bag I set out to trudge uphill in the noon day sun. The track deteriorated about half way up and became a bit "climby", but eminently passable until I got to the hole in the hill which allows you to go from the marina side of the rock to the other side of the rock.

Figure 27 The hand dug tunnel of the 18th Cent.

This tunnel was dug/excavated by soldiers in the late 18th century to provide all round visibility for the local garrison, so that they be made aware of the approach of Napoleon's fleet, and /or the British fleet. Anyway, I struggled through the rock strewn tunnel and hit the other side. Where suddenly this massive blast of wind hit me. I had been climbing the leeward side of the hill and was now on the windward side of the hill and there was quite a difference, I struggled forward, ever upward until I saw that a landslide had removed most of the path, and in these conditions I made an executive decision to retreat in good order and find a bar.

The following day I took a taxi to the local 9 hole golf course and was able to get 18 holes in before 16:00 hrs. I was a bit surprised that there wasn't anyone else out on the course at all. I was told later that everyone else was asleep, as the temperature was above thirty degrees. Members of the Golf Club, were mostly but not exclusively British, and they all started arriving as I finished my round. Oh well.

The next day it was time to leave Calpe and head for Villejoyoza, with twelve knots on the nose, along with hazy sunshine and a slight swell, we motored on. On our way we passed the Towers of Benidorm, similar to the Towers of Babel but with more swimming pools. Benidorm does not have a marina at all, otherwise I would have put in there just to say I had visited it. We never got any closer than half a mile. I did not feel I had missed anything too important.

Figure 28 The Ilfach Golf Course with the previously climbed Penon in the background

We arrived at Villajoyosa and found it to be very "joyous" and "jolly". This was the first time we became conscious of so many Brits in the area, as most of the restos in the marina seemed to cater more for British tastes, albeit the culinary tastes of the '70.s and 80,s. (As we travel South and West of Villajoyosa, the Brit component of the places we visit just keeps on increasing. I think we have left the more Spanish part behind, which is ironic as the Catalonians do not consider themselves "Spanish" but a separate entity "Catalonian")

We stayed two nights and then left for Alicante with all sails out, but in a light rain containing Saharan sand. This manifested as leaving red stains all over the deck and we weren't going fast enough and the sea was not rough enough to wash the decks down, so it stayed red & gritty until we got to a water tap. Like many places in France, the Spanish marinas do not like you using their valuable drinking water allowance to wash down a boat, even tho' we saw many Spaniards doing this, it is still frowned upon by officials. Particularly if you are a foreign registered boat.

Figure 29 Valencia to Alicante

Chapter 10
ALICANTE TO CARTAGENA

We stayed in Alicante for four nights, visiting the Cathedral and the Basilica, both very beautiful in a Gothic way. Here we saw the effect of the British raid on Alicante in 1765, manifest by the many holes in the sea facing wall as well as a cannon ball stuck into the wall that surrounds the town. For some reason, no-one has set fit to remove it yet, or repair the holes we caused. I was surprised it had stayed this way for that long.

Figure 30 Town wall with English shot still embedded in it

As we approached the Cathedral of St Nicholas via a medium sized plaza, I noticed some strange patterns in the blocks of stone, which I recognised from a similar church in France, which had been used by the Nazis in late 1944 to subdue the resistance there. Looking at the patterns, most of the "disturbances" were at top-chest and head height. I then realised this was a firing squad plaza with the church front as "back stop". It had been used to prevent the rounds going any further. But they did chip away at the soft sandstone used to build the church in the 17th Century.

Figure 31 Alicante cathedral with the marks of the firing squads from 1939

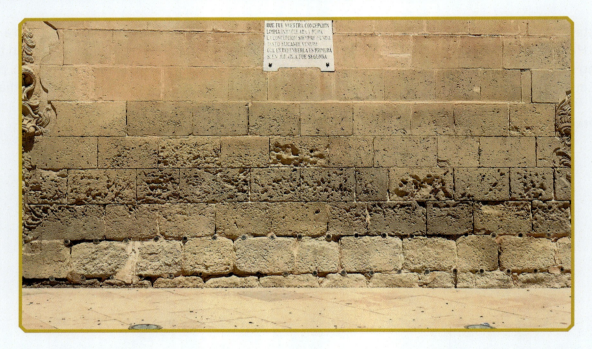

Obviously, there was very little written about this in the Cathedral or on the tourist plaques in the square but further analysis when I returned to England, told me that Alicante was one of the last places in Andalusia to be captured by Franco's forces, and many had tried to escape with the help of a Welshman called Archibald Dickson. It is a sobering thought that he was able to help only 2600 people out of the 250,000 who applied for his help, and that he could take no more because his ship was well overloaded (it was only a small tramp steamer) and it was he who piloted the last steamer out of Alicante harbour, past the Nationalist forces under cover of darkness. He is acknowledged to have saved more than 2600 people, but many of the rest, comprising a large proportion of them, perished in the plaza of the cathedral.

Figure 32 The statue of Archibald Dixon on the side of Alicante Harbour

Archibald Dixon is considered a British Hero in the environs of Alicante but is hardly known in England or indeed in Wales. There is a statue to him in Alicante port and every year, the local people on the anniversary of the end of the Civil War honour his name with a garland put around his statue. His ship the SS Stanbrook was torpedoed in late 1939 at the beginning of the war with the Nazis and she went down with all twenty two hands, including Archibald.

The next day it was off to the local Sevriano Ballesteros Golf course, by local train. Once again it was more than thirty degrees, but as an extra, there was a 5-800m walk between each hole, just to make it more interesting (and a bit more knackering). This was a tough course to play but with one VERY interesting hole. On the 14th there were the remains of a Roman Villa right in the middle of the fairway. It turns out that when they were laying out the course they came across the remains of a large Roman Villa and after full archaeological mapping and examination, Seve decided to integrate them into the hole as a "special hazard", and for me, it certainly was, I lost two balls trying to cross it.

Figure 33 Hole 14 An ancient monument ball trap

The following day it was time to climb to the Castle above Alicante known as the Castello de Santa Barbera, which I found very sterile and over-restored, but the views were impressive. Then we went off to visit the town itself. Which we did, checking out the Basilica this time, as well as the local wine. All this enjoyment had to end soon, and our travels just had to continue. The next day we were off to Torrevieja.

Torrevieja, is also known as the Costa del Yorkshire, as it has the largest density of Brits, Germans and Scandis on the whole Spanish coast. Several Spaniards live here too – it is where they keep their second homes. Apart from a lovely beach and a good marina, there is not much else to do here. So I cleaned the log and changed the filters on the holding tank breathers. These filters do not have a "change by" date, but intuition told me it was the right time. Either that or it was the gentle all pervading sewage niff. Torrevieja is also famous for fitting 64 amp fittings into all its berths.

A small diversion on Power fittings

Figure 34 How not to design a power adapter sequence

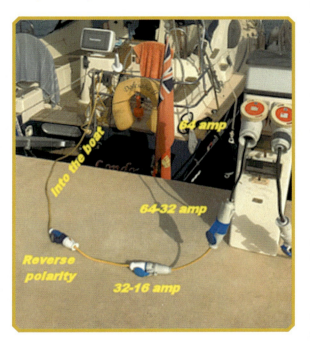

Most yachts (inc. Dofesaba II) work on a standard 16 amp plug, and to be fair, MOST European marinas and ports will have these as standard on the shore. However many motor boats are more power hungry than sailing yachts when in port, as they have AC.s to run, so they require a 32 amp plug. In most marinas these will be put on the larger berths, sometimes with a complimentary 16 amp fitting, so you have the choice. Alternatively, you can fit up an adaptor yourself as I have done, or the Capitania will hire you one for the duration of your stay. Many superyachts will require a 64 amp fitting, but as these superyachts usually have their own berthing area, to keep us peasants away from the owners and their crews, they are rarely seen. Consequently one is unlikely to buy a 64 amp adapter (In fact, in all our meanderings so far, this was the first and only time I saw a 64 amp fitting). So in Torrevieja with its strange decision to fit 64 amp fittings everywhere including for even a 24 foot berth, one had to hire an adapter at vast cost and inconvenience. Not only that, but once I connected them all, I found the polarity was reversed, so I had to add in a polarity reversal adaptor.

Eventually my power take-off looked like as shown in the photo. What a palaver, but it had to be done.

After Torrevieja it was a nice sail down to the entrance of the Mar Menor. We arrived a bit early and had to wait for the bridge to open. All the time we watched hundreds of small power vessels screaming down the canal into the playground of the Mar Menor while we waited for the road bridge to open. It was a Saturday, blazing hot and the Spanish were out for a play on the water. We had been wanting to visit here for many years having heard what a lovely peaceful place it was. The water was only 6m deep, it was totally sheltered, so sheltered that there were many sailing, diving, parasailing, kayaking etc. schools up and down the inland coasts. I was looking for some nice quiet anchoring without bouncy swell to show Mary how lovely all this sailing lark really was. We were intending to stay a week or longer. I had picked out an anchorage at the far south of the Mar Menor near Playa Honda as the wind was coming from the south and we would be protected by the land, even though it was low lying.

Figure 35 Entrance (and exit) to the Mar Menor

As we went into the Mar Menor and under the bridge, some light cloud appeared, visible in the photo, but by the time we had transited the canal it had started to blow sixteen knots. We had two hours to get to the anchorage and in that time the wind picked up to twenty four knots and the swell increased. Down went the hook and appeared to set nicely. So off with the engine, all squared away and down for a cup of tea.

I then looked out of the window "Mary - We are going sideways" Down goes the tea, on go the instruments and engine, and up comes the anchor with a massive ball of weed, this explained why we were not attached to the floor. It took Mary quite a bit of effort to clear, and away we went. The weather is still howling and the 'oh so calm' sea, was not.

I decided to go and hide behind one of the two islands that we had spotted on our way down to the South of the Mar Menor, which, even then, were sheltering five vessels. We decided to hide behind the largest island in three metres of water and twenty metres of chain, just to make sure. We felt a lot safer but it was quite bumpy. Before we turned in that night (wind still >twenty four knots) I looked around the anchorage to see that we were the only ones left. I did not inform the crew.

In the morning the wind had dropped to five knots and all had settled down nicely, but we felt that it had been spoiled for us and we decided to continue our journey and anchor in the Cabo Palos anchorage, as that was even more sheltered than our previously planned anchorage near Playa Honda. Turns out that Cabo Palos anchorage was two Miles directly due East of Playa Honda but the advantage was a whopping great hill up wind of us. We arrived in gentle breezes and anchored first time. Then off to the beach café for a beer and a wander on the beach. I took a walk over the other side of the hill to see what the Marina was like. First, as I breasted the rise, I got hit by the very strong wind, straight into the face, which was quite a surprise, and when I got down to the marina, I found that it was totally full and I saw a small yacht

Figure 36 Map of the journey around the Mar Menor

of 32 ft was being turned away. We later saw him making for the Mar Menor.

We spent a peaceful night rocking gently at anchor. We shared the anchorage with four other boats all night, but were last to leave in the morning, as we were on our way to the very famous city of Cartagena.

The wind was fourteen knots "up the chuff", a well-used sailing expression to mean that the wind was coming from directly behind the boat, which on many vessels can be a most dangerous point of sail, because if not handled correctly the boom can "Gybe" or suddenly swing from all the way out on the port side to all the way out on the starboard side in one very swift movement. Should a head or any other part of the body be in the way of the sheer momentum of ½ ton of aluminium, steel and sailcloth, then a lot of damage can be done, not only to the human head but more importantly (in my opinion) to the rigging.

We are fortunate on Dofesaba II that we have several mitigating factors to minimise danger -

The cockpit floor is quite deep.

We are both quite short, such that the boom flies just above my head (only just)

We have a swinging jib, with mini preventers on both sides (the unused spinnaker guys being used wisely) so we always have control if required.

On Dofesaba II the swinging the jib goes across at 175 deg and the boom at 185 deg, so the helmsman (ie Me) has a fair amount of warning that a Gybe is imminent.

Mary & I practise gybing regularly, so we both know what to do.

We were able to sail all the way to Cartagena. Entering the port is quite a sight as it is a natural harbour with an oil terminal on the starboard side, a cruise ship terminal dead ahead and a freight port off to the port side. Our destination was the marina, the other side of the Cruise ship terminal. As we entered, my eyes were drawn to the large gun emplacements on either shore.

Figure 37 Guardians of Cartagena

These housed four inch naval guns supplied by England to the Spanish Republican Govt and were used to keep out Nationalist naval forces. They did the job, until Franco's forces came up behind them from the land side. A bit like Singapore in 1941. The gun emplacements are all still there, but unfortunately not the guns (nor any ammunition – which would be very interesting)

We were assigned our berth and tied up. We spent several days visiting the marine archaeological museum, all the big churches, the loveliest Roman Theatre in Spain, the Amphitheatre, the bath houses and AT LAST a museum of the Civil War, some acknowledgement that it had existed. Albeit very small and housed in a bomb shelter. Few people realise that it was not only Guernica that was bombed, many Spanish cities suffered aerial bombardment by Fascist forces, and very few were prepared for it.

Figure 38 The wonderful Roman Theatre in Central Cartagena

After a weeks sightseeing we decided to leave the boat in Cartagena and return to the UK for two weeks holiday.

So there will now be an intermission and time for an ice cream.

Figure 39 Alicante to Cartagena

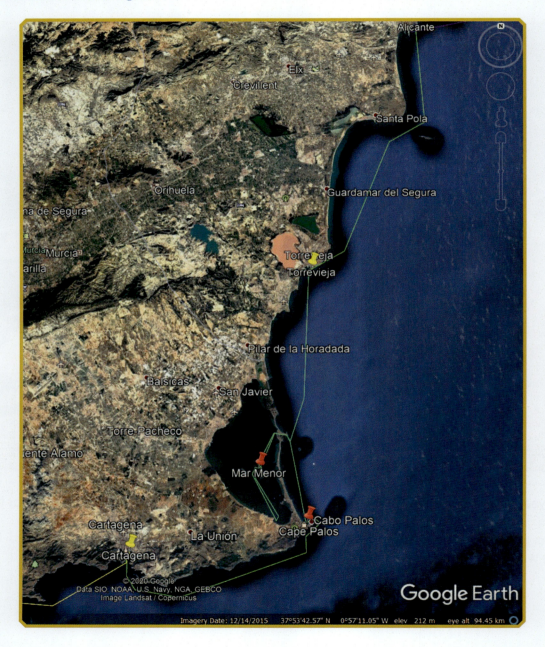

Chapter 11
CARTAGENA TO CABO DE GATO

We returned to Cartagena after two weeks ready to sail the ocean main again. It was now noticeably hotter, with a minimum temperature in the cabin of thirty deg. after 10:00 hrs every day. We rested in Cartagena for a day and then set off on our travels.

Our next stop was Mazzaron, where we did some washing and very little else, and then pressed on to an anchorage by the Cabo de Cope. This was another one where hiding behind a big hill was a good idea. On shore was a very strange looking castle type thing – that was very unprepossessing and it was all alone, surrounded by farmland and nothing else, just a small beach and a road down to it. We stayed on board and left in the morning. It turns out that we had parked right in an old Phoenician port that had become disused during the 15th Cent. when the local mines gave out. Up until that time the port at Cabo de Cope had been the main loading base for Zinc, Silver, Lead and Gold. During the 11th Cent. The local lord had built the strange castle to protect the port and it had managed to survive all this time – I suppose that was because it was now so isolated.

Figure 40 The actual castle and its model in the Museum

However there was nothing on the ground to show the port had been there at all. I only found this information out when I visited the local museum in Aguilas (our next stop) and there was the funny shaped castle in a model of the coast as it had been in the 11th Cent. With comments about it all (mostly in Spanish but I was getting quite good at translating, most of it).

After that it was on to Aguilas where I visited the museum of archaeology (see above). Climbed a big hill to look at the fort there (St Joan de Montiel) – pretty normal fort, but by now I was getting a bit blasé about forts and cannons and all that archaeology stuff as I had seen so many.

We left Aguilas the next day heading for Garucha, with steady twelve to eighteen knot winds from the starboard quarter. After several hours we arrived at the port to find it almost deserted, consequently with loads of space. We hailed the marineros who guided us into a berth and then both of them failed to catch the well thrown lines, then they picked up the wrong lazy lines for us to pull to the front, all in all, a very poor performance which we found very unusual, as normally the Spanish marineros were experienced and competent, but it looked like Garrucha was the exception that proves the rule.

We didn't stay very long and left Garrucha on our way to San Jose, our last stop before the infamous Cabo de Gato. San Jose was quite a small port and I had been advised to call ahead, which obviously I did, and I was told merrily that there was a place for me. After such reassurance we set off happily to San Jose at 08:30 hrs in a freshening wind with lots of West in it.

Unfortunately this meant that it was thirty degrees off our head with the swell left over from last night's strong winds, dead on the nose. This made progress slow and uncomfortable. After nearly six hours we were very pleased to see the entrance of San Jose. Actually we couldn't see the entrance, as it was facing West and we were coming in almost directly from the East, but we could see the walls of the harbour and that was good enough to boost our mood. As we turned around the mole to come into the harbour, I got my first good look at our refuge, and then fully realised how small the port actually was. As I approached the only quay, so as to come in sideways-to as advised by the Capitainia, a Belgian flagged boat was just leaving the quay, I said "Hello" but received a very grumpy reply and a filthy look (In Belgian – so I didn't understand it) however as I was too preoccupied in coming in to the quay, I thought no more about it.

Figure 41 The only large berth in town

We tied up first time (quite an achievement as we had not side-too moored for over three months) and went to offer our papers to the Capitania. The cost was very small and she (The Capitania) was very helpful and was chuckling to herself. When I asked why, she explained that the Belgians had come in earlier and moored up on the quay without asking or talking to the Capitania or the Marineros, which miffed the local folk quite a bit. They had tried to explain to the skipper that the berth was booked and he had to move, but as he claimed he did not speak Spanish and they did not speak the particular Belgian dialect that he did, they had to go and find an Englishman locally who could talk English to the Belgian as theirs was not good enough to persuade the recalcitrant Belgian to "Go Away". This took several hours and said

Belgian had only just agreed to Foxtrot Oscar with very bad grace, just as I turned into the port at exactly the right moment (or wrong moment; depending on one's position in the argument).

When I returned to the boat, we noticed several other vessels now anchoring in the lee of the harbour, some quite big. It turns out there was only 1 visitor's mooring available for a boat longer than 32 feet and I had nabbed it by having the forethought and politeness to phone ahead and try to speak Spanish. Huzzah! Sometimes I amaze myself.

We stayed in San Jose for 2 nights as we prepared ourselves mentally & physically for the Cabo de Gato. The departure time arrived and we said farewell and set off. The route was not difficult, head South, turn right, come level with the cape, turn half right and keep going 'til you hit the shore. All being well that should be Aguadulce. While doing that, check the wind coming from behind, avoid going too close to the shore and prepare to batten down when rounding the cape – oh and beware, the wind can change at any moment.

As we were making our way to Aguadulce we came upon another British flagged boat, called *Deep Blue* doing the same. We said hello on VHF and agreed to meet up when we landed. Four and half hours after setting off we arrived at Aquadulce to find everything was closed until 17:00, so we tied up to the visitor's quay along with everyone else and had a cold beer. Just then *Deep Blue* turned up and tied alongside us, and that was an excuse for another one.

Eventually, a marinero directed us to a berth deep within what was a pretty big marina, and away we went to it. I had rather rashly offered to go into a "standard" 12x4m berth on the basis we were only just over 12m long and only just over 4m wide and to be honest I was getting fed up paying the extra dosh for a 15m x 5m berth when I didn't really need it. So I was a little surprised to find that the berth I had been allocated was directly opposite a quay jutting out with boats attached to it that made it a very tight squeeze.

"Oh well" I thought "better put your money where your big mouth is", so I lined myself up and put her into reverse, slowly but surely with judicious touches on the bow thruster controls. I started with the bowsprit about thirty cm. (one foot) from the boat ahead, then into reverse, came in at an angle of 45 deg, then once the starboard quarter was nearly lined up between the two boats either side of my berth, I slid the stern in along side the bow of the starboard boat until the port quarter got close to the port boat then bunged the head around with the bow thruster and slid gently back to the concrete without touching a thing. We tied the boat up, had a beer and I set off with to find Deep Blue.

As I got off the boat and was walking down the quay an Englishman hailed me.

"I say, have you just come in on that Southerly"

"Yes I have" said I, thinking he wanted to ask me about Southerlys and lifting keels and other things nautical, as does happen.

"May I just say what a remarkable piece of boat handling that was"

Well you could have knocked me down with a feather – I was gob smacked (or Bouche Frapped, as the French might say) so much so, that for a second I could not think of anything to say, let alone something polite and apposite.

"errrr…. Well thank you" was all I could stammer out,

"No-one has ever said that before"

It was true, I am sure I am not unique as a skipper in thinking that I can handle a boat as well as the next man, and I believe my skills are pretty good, but that was the first time that anyone else has even noticed, let alone openly commented on it so positively, an extremely rare occurrence. There is a possibility that he was completely drunk and had no clue about what he was looking at, or talking about, but I decided he was a rarely found man of great intelligence and perspicacity and he really did know what he was talking about. Anyway it made me feel better.

We stayed three nights and during that time I took a car trip with the crew of *Deep Blue* out to Fort Bravo and then a bus ride into Almeria to the Cathedral and the Alcazabar which is another Moorish castle built to defend the local ports.

A small diversion on Fort Bravo –

Deep Blue is sailed by Andrew & Bea, and Andrew has always wanted to visit the film set used by the Spaghetti Westerns (The Good, The Bad & The Ugly, along with many more).

We hired a car and they invited me along. The film set was abandoned back in the 1980's and converted into a "tourist attraction" with daily playlets in the Saloon bar.

Figure 42 Main street in Fort Bravo

Then a resurgent film industry wanted to use the sets again, so the site looks after tourists and films and has a living set of livery stables to provide horses for cowboy films and while not filming, they are hired out for people to ride. The sets, both American cowboy town and Mexican pueblo town are located within Europe's only official desert, which you have seen many times in films, as it is very similar in aspect to parts of Hollywood, well the desert parts anyway.

The following day I played a round at the Almerimar golf course, but it was not very exciting and I didn't play well so we will move on to the following day when we left Aguadulce for Almerimar.

Figure 43 Cartagena to the Cabo de Gato

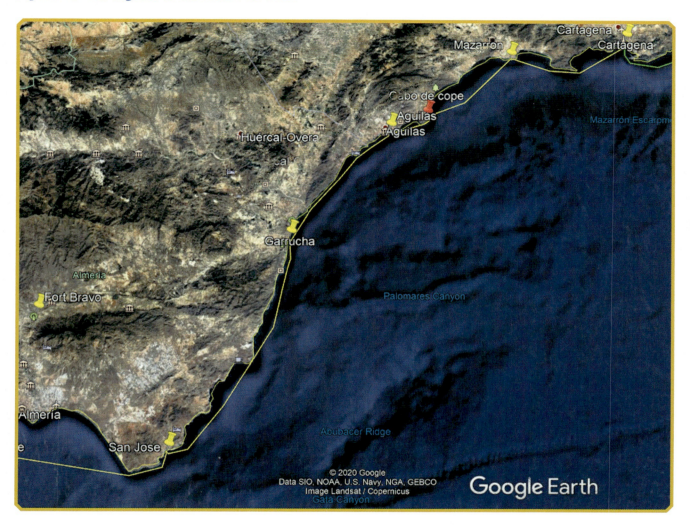

Chapter 12
CABO DE GATO TO BENALMADENA

We spent five hours sailing in seventeen to twenty knots of wind and a slight swell. As the wind was on my 180, or even directly behind, I thought I would be clever and laid a course so as to steer to my 170 for an hour and then my 190, so giving ten degrees off the wind. This method, although it takes slightly longer was a lot safer as it reduced the chance of an accidental or "crash" gybe. The downside was that every now and then we had to Gybe. This is something the crew and I had practiced, so I was not unduly worried. You will be pleased to hear that we did six perfect gybes, safely and securely without any stress to skipper, crew or the boat. When we arrived in Almerimar it was a surprise to feel the full force of the wind, because now as we turned into the port (after Sails down and Engine on) we had the full force of the wind coming from the front of the vessel. This made berthing a bit tricky, compounded with one of the marineros giving the wrong lazy line to me. We were also advised to put out a mid-ships or bow tether to hold the boat against the strong wind. So we did.

A small diversion on downwind sailing – (for the interested non-sailor) Sailing itself is not a dangerous sport, however there is always the possibility of falling overboard and drowning or being hit by the boom causing you to fall overboard and drown, or just sustain a nasty head injury, so being aware of the boom and where it is going and the speed it will be moving at, is of primary concern to all skippers. When sailing downwind it is easy to think that the wind is not very strong and this is due to the apparent wind effect. With a twenty knot wind and the boat going at seven knots in the same direction (as in "downwind") one feels the effect of a thirteen knot wind. However when one turns into the wind, for instance to furl the sails or even to turn onto a different course, it is then that the apparent wind becomes up to twenty seven knots. This is why a wind speed indicator is always visible from the cockpit, and a very valuable tool it is.

Almerimar is a completely false building concept. Previous to the seventies there was nothing there. Ernest McAlpine wanted somewhere in Spain to take his family that included a sports centre, a Golf course, Sun & Sand. Unfortunately for him at that time (1975) that sort of resort did not exist, so being a building entrepreneur, he decided to build one. The marina has one VERY large berth (for his personal yacht) it includes one very large family house, called the McAlpine mansion, a hotel with several pools, all surrounding a shaped marina which is populated by four storey apartment blocks, where the ground floor are shops, which are mainly bars, with the odd chandlery and a clothes shop or two. And here's the rub, nearly all of it is owned by the English. ALL the bars do Spanish beer but also Bacon & Eggs for breakfast. The main cuisine is as if you were back in 1975 - EVERYTHING is in English first and if Spanish is used, it is second. I found it very surreal, I expected to see notices on the doors saying "Ay Habla Espanol" (Here we speak Spanish) As there was nothing to see, I played a round at the Golf Course (Again – I was not very good – but it was thirty seven degrees) and we then moved on.

The next day was a seven hour sail, in swell with the winds gusting fifteen to twenty knots Again the wind was on my 180 and again we gybed a few times, but not as often as the previous voyage. Six hours into the voyage with Motril harbour in sight, but very faint on the horizon, and as we were just pootling along, I saw something strange in the water dead ahead, right on the nose even. I decided on a judicious movement of the wheel and so avoided a floating fridge freezer. As it floated past at six knots I thought to myself.

"That looks quite dangerous particularly for a thin skinned fast traveling sport boat" (which to be fair we had seen many of during our journey from Almerimar). I sat quietly and debated with myself and eventually decided that I had better do what I considered to be the right thing. I reached for the VHF radio handset, checked it was on Channel 16 and called in a "Securite".

For the uninitiated this is a low level message warning ships of a problem in the position indicated. I knew that there was a Spanish Coastguard at Cabo de Gato (see pages earlier) and that they, and everyone else were monitoring Channel 16 (Hence my hesitation, I really didn't want to get it wrong). So after I had done that, my conscience became clearer and I only hope the Spanish Coastguard did something about it, I had done my bit.

Figure 44   Motril cathedral on top of an 8th cent mosque

As I entered the harbour at Motril the wind gusted to over thirty knots so I was pleased to see three marineros come to help us in. You often get the feeling that Spanish Marineros are used to incompetent Englishmen, or maybe just incompetent yachties of any nationality as they are always surprised when someone shows that a boat can be handled well without smashing, swearing and stress. I put this down to my competent crew. (God, I hope she reads this)

Motril harbour and marina is about three km from the ancient Phoenician town of Motril itself. So it was a nice bus ride off to see the Cathedral on the hill, dedicated to the Virgin Mary, which had been built on top of a Nazrid Mosque, and after that to visit the Motril museum. We dined that night in their lovely Club Nautico. (Not all Club Nauticos are very good, but this one was worthy of mention).

The following day in the wind and rain we went to the only Sugar cane museum and Rummery left in the area. For centuries, the flat plains from the sea to the foothills were covered in Sugar Cane plantations, and canals to move the cut cane down to the processing plants of which today there is only one left called Ron Montero, (Which is very famous throughout Europe, but virtually unheard of in UK) which we dutifully examined and tried several of their products, which is all that was expected of us and we couldn't let them down. Then it was a Taxi back to the boat for a gentle lie down.

On the following day we decided to take it easy as the wind was below six knots and very slightly off the nose, however to make it more exciting we decided to anchor next to the Cabo de los Canuelos. This was a beautifully sheltered bay with two beach restos. So it was out with the dinghy and into the shore, not a very long journey I will admit.

Figure 45 The beach at Cabo de Canuelos (from the Restaurant)

This was followed by a light snack for lunch and then a lie on the beach until time to dinghy back and onto the boat for dinner, all safe & snugly. Once again, we were all alone at the anchorage. I did begin to wonder, was it us?.

The next morning, we were off at 10:00 hrs. The water was so clear I could see quite clearly that the anchor had dragged, but only ten metres, however it was a sobering thought. The journey was not a long one and as we sailed down the coast, we passed beach after beach with rows of deck chairs and a bar in the background, but I chose not to stop, there is only so much a man can do to help the local tourist industry.

As we entered the harbour of Calleta de Vellez it became obvious that things here were going to be a little tight, and as we turned, up popped the wind. Unfortunately, I believed the chart when it said there was three metres depth in the harbour, even though I knew this was likely to be wrong, or at least "out of date". As we ventured down alongside one pontoon ready to reverse into the selected berth, there was a clunk as I hit one of the concrete blocks used to attach the lazy lines to. I then threw the boat into reverse, the wind blew and we drifted near to several vessels picking up one of the lazy lines with the keel and stopping the boat from going backwards, so I had to go forwards to disconnect the line from the keel, as I did this, there was another clonk (albeit a small one) showed I had once again connected with the concrete block, now it was time to wind the keel up, which to be fair I should have done as I entered the harbour. To no avail. Lots of whirring noise to show the pump was trying, but no upping of the keel. This was not good. Anyway I managed to berth without further issues, but no matter what I did, I could not move the keel. The local boatyard would not lift me out, as they had too many fishing boats to service, so I put off dealing with the problem "until later", and went for a refreshing de-stressing beer.

A SMALL DIVERSION ON WHY CALLETA DE VELLEZ

We were aiming for Calleta de Vellez for several good reasons, and none of them nautical. In 2010, my wife/crew decided that she had had enough of me telling her that her Yoga practice was not tough enough for men. (I know, I was younger then) and she then booked us on the only Yoga retreat in Southern Spain that allowed a beer and wine with the meal. In my mind a sure sign of civilisation. The Ashram was way up in the hills just down from a hill top village called Comares. This was an old Moorish town semi isolated. It was surrounded by orange groves, dusty forests and rocks. The local sounds were the plashing of the spring, goat's bells and barking dogs. Saluting the sun as it rose above the ocean while 1000m up a mountain at 07:00 hrs was surprisingly magical. Anyway to cut a ramble much shorter, the local beach was Torre del Mar and next to it was the Port of Calleta de Vellez, a well known fishing harbour, and definitely not designed for your average yachtie. We returned to the Ashram every year for 5 years so by 2018 we knew the area quite well, and we had often promised ourselves that one day we would sail into Calleta and THEN go up to see the Ashram.

So we did. We left the boat in the port and hired a car and then we drove up the mountain to say 'Hello' to Les the yoga teacher, only to find he had sold up and gone. This was a bit of a surprise but we recovered enough to to say "Hello" to the current owner, who was also a Yoga teacher, but she was one of these true believers, and combined yoga with healthy nutrients and body purging, definitely no alcohol, beach visits, shopping or trips to the local café. Well we were not having any of that, so we bid farewell to that part of our life and returned to the sea. But not before a swift café in our favourite restaurant/bar in Comares, where we used to walk to on our daily excursions – for a cheeky beer and coffee.

Every life should have some disappointments. To cheer ourselves up we went for fresh sardines cooked on the beach in Torre del Mar.

Figure 46   Sardines on the beach at Torre del Mar - caught that morning

The following day was Sunday and time to visit the Caves of Nerja. These we had heard of many times but never visited, so it was time.

The caves contain some of the oldest cave paintings in Europe and I was eager to visit them and I also like a nice piece of rock. So when we turned up to be told the cave paintings were inaccessible, due to restoration work, but lots of rock was available to look at, I was a tad disappointed, but we had to go in anyway. After that, it was lunch with some old friends who lived in the area, and this was considered by all to be a pleasant way to spend a day, in a resto with a beer, in the sunshine, on the beach; what was not to like.

Figure 47 An example from the caves at Nerja

It was time to prepare for our final voyage for 2019, so we said goodbye to Calleta by entering the two metre swell directly outside the port. As I turned onto our course, we realised that the wind was coming from the same direction as the swell, which is not uncommon but annoying. Wind and swell against us – what a final voyage this turned out to be. Five bumpy hours later we entered the Benalmadena "complex".

Benalmadena is another of those complexes built for the "edification of the British tourist". A big marina, lots of apartments surrounding the big marina, with boat services (cleaning, fixing, buying & selling, chandler – you name it) and lots of restos. ALL of them fronted by Englishmen, except the one next to us, which was fronted by a Glaswegian – which I doubt any Spaniard would have understood. Because we had booked early, we apparently were given a prime berth, and it was, carefully nestled beneath four-story apartments sheltered from the wind and most of the sun, right outside the restaurants. We must have been polite to all the Capitanias on our way down the coast. I am convinced they all talk to each other and mark you up or down based on your behaviour, otherwise it would be too much of a coincidence.

Figure 48 Dofesaba II snugly berthed with a friend to talk to.

However this is the end of the line for us within this story. We left several days later and returned to the UK via Cordoba and Malaga, knowing the vessel was safe and would be ready for next May when the whole cycle will start again.

So look out for "The Adventures of Dofesaba II 2020" which should be coming soon. I hope you enjoyed the narrative and that this might even encourage you to visit the East coast of Spain, as we can highly recommend it.

Figure 49 Cabo de Gato to Benalmadena

Some Statistics

Days at sea/in port	107
Miles	364
Engine hours	98
Hours underway	156
Sailing Hours	58 – 37%
Ports visited	32
Anchorages used	7

Note : All pictures taken with an iPhone7 copyright PJBell. All maps from Google Earth

Preface to the second part of the book.

As you have read above, the plan for 2020 was to re-start our adventures in May from Benalmadena and continue all the way round to the Rias of NE Spain in one season. It was not to be, a deadly virus put paid to our plans.

In the grand scheme of things delaying a holiday for two mostly retired folk does not in any way compare to the postponement of weddings, the poor way funerals of loved ones was handled and the deaths of so many people, including those selfless care workers, Doctors and Nurses who unfortunately succumbed, terminally to the effects of the Virus. And not to forget those that recovered and still live with the effects.

Then there is all the people who lost their jobs, livelihoods and sadly their relationships due to this deadly disease. Writing this in December 2020 I can only hope the situation has improved with the current promise of at least three worthwhile vaccines almost ready for distribution.

However this book is written to give you a lift and fill your heart with humour and the joy of adventure, albeit second hand, so I will not mention the Virus again, except in passing.

Chapter 13
ESCAPING THE VIRUS

We escaped from the UK in mid-July knowing there was a possibility we would be quarantined on our way back – but it had to be done. I took a week preparing the boat in the yard in Benalmadena and we set sail on the 28th July for the West.

We spent a terrible night. Mary was too hot and I compressed my spinal discs by trying to carry too much in one suitcase back from the supermarket, such that a "touch of the old problem" rears its ugly head. I get a bit of sciatica that affects the nerves. The pain is as if I have been kicked in the left buttock – by Norman Hunter. (those too young to know this archetypal left back for Leeds and England need to go look it up on that t'internet thang) anyway it is annoyingly uncomfortable, particularly when trying to sleep. I completely failed to do that and dozed til dawn. At 08:30 hrs I jumped up and made some tea, then went off to get the boat ready.

A small diversion on decision making within marriage and on a boat

On a ship the Skippers word is final – this is encapsulated in Tradition. Note I said Skipper not Captain – A Captain's word and decision is backed up by Maritime Law. So if the Captain says "pull that line" and the crew doesn't and we sink and cause loss of life, it is not the Captain's fault. Unfortunately, a Skipper is not in such a controlled position.

It would be lovely if I said to my crew "Tomorrow we are leaving at 07:00 hours – you must be ready". and we left at 07:00 hrs and everyone was ready. Bearing in mind I have checked the weather, sorted the route, phoned ahead for a berth etc. – done lots of skippery things.

What actually happens is –

"We shall leave tomorrow at 07:00 hrs"

"Oh no, that is way too early, I cannot be ready by then"

"Well you may have to be – tide, weather, waiting for no man nor woman etc."

"Oh no, can we make it 10:00?– I am sure I will be ready by then and I will feel so much better"

Well as you can imagine – not everything works the way a Skipper wants, so we compromised on 09:45 – this we call marriage.

We did leave exactly at 09:45 and off we trolled into a hazy Spanish morning. It was already twenty five deg. C. and the haze promised more. I put up my improvised Bimini to get as much shade as possible, opened up the front of the spray hood to get as much through draught as possible and set the controls for the heart of the sun – or even 'towards Marbella'.

Figure 50 Dofesaba II in Marbella - A dreary port

It was at that moment I realised that the autopilot was showing 'no pilot, no pilot' – a little cryptic I thought – This is what we call an "Oh Dear" moment – 'cos if we could not run on autopilot then someone has to steer – obviously; and I had lots of stuff to do and Mary is not very confident steering. I had a quick look around – then asked Mary to steer while I went downstairs to check.

"Why don't you steer which you're better at, and I will go and cycle all the electronics as I am ok with doing that" says the crew.

So you see how the skippers word is treated as LAW on our boat. However she made a very good point which I had to concede while I meekly took the helm. Down she went – then two seconds later

"Would it help if I turn the autopilot switch to 'ON'"

"Well darling, it certainly won't do any harm" says I and lo – there be a working autopilot. Now, before we get into the blame game – it was oi that dunnit – er... I freely admit I didn't turn on the Autopilot. I have no idea why – I just did not turn it on. When my lovely wife did – all worked wonderfully and the tide of trepidation building in my breast was removed.

We trundled for the next four hours. I was interested in what affect the massive amount of work I had done on the underneath of the hull in Benalmadena was having. It became time for a little investigation. I knew that last year that at exactly 2000 rpm we got 5.9 to 6.0 knots log speed. So I reset the throttle to EXACTLY 2000 rpm and looked at the log. 6.0, 6.1, then touching 6.2 only to hover between 6.1 & 6.2 for the next ten minutes.

So I had spent €1400 for a maximum 0.2 knots extra speed. Well - that was worth it.

Figure 51 The cleanest shiniest prop and hull you ever did see

A small diversion on statistics

Statistics are there to prove any point you wish to make. They do not have to really exist or to be quoted verbatim, as long as you say them loudly enough. To be fair I have been a little disingenuous in the previous paragraph. Comparing a completely cleaned boat with the way I left it last year. Because – last year the boat had been used daily and there had been very little chance for much weed or barnacles to build up so while the hull was not clean, it certainly wasn't that dirty either. During September 2019 to July 2020 (almost 9 months) the boat had been sitting in sea water. I assumed there was weed and barnacle build up on the hull, and if I had not cleaned it, all that rubbish would have surely reduced my progress through the water. This was one of the jobs done at Benalmadena.

Chapter 14
ARRIVING IN ESTEPONA

Leaving Marbella we soon arrived at Estepona. We had been trying to get to Estepona to see some friends that we last saw in 2007/8 at a Seismic Conference. Unfortunately as it was so long ago neither of us could remember which one it was. We spent two lovely evenings with them, one as guests in their distinctive apartment block, so distinctive that we had noticed it as we crept along the coast.

Figure 52 a rare sight at Sea

After several days we left Estepona in two knot winds, which increased to five knots directly behind us – I sighed and left the sails furled, as even a five knot wind is not enough to propel us through the water. When you think about it, if you are standing still with all sails out, then five knots will propel us to about two and a half knots, but once you get to two and a half knots the relative wind drops to two and a half knots and that isn't enough for more than one knot. So a delicate balance of around two knots can be achieved if you are lucky. With the weight we carry (>fourteen tons) this becomes more like one point seven knots. The skipper decides it is hardly worth getting the sails out so we continue with the iron topsail on.

As we trundle along, the sea mist comes down and so on goes the Radar and our automatic Fog Horn. We can hear the local fog horns booming out across the sea. The Radar shows many echoes – far more than seems normal. We keep a sharp look out. On the starboard quarter is a disturbance on the sea surface, is it a bit of wind? – should I put the sails out? Er... no! it is a pod of porpoises about 60-100 strong sliding through the water leisurely, yet purposefully (well they would, wouldn't they) they did not deviate their path in any way just went a bit deeper when our boat got in their way. 'Well that was nice' we said and then fifteen minutes later another pod went by. Were they dolphins as the locals liked to insist. Well they were only one to one and a half metres long and that is pretty small for a Dolphin but about right for a harbour porpoise. And no, they weren't all juveniles.

On we went nervously checking up front with the mark one eyeball and the Radar, when out of the merk, several huge ships appeared. The mist lifted and we found ourselves in the midst of a ship park. Tankers, Cargo vessels and 3 mighty Stena Drill ships – which normally charge about a million dollars a day just to exist. I tried to imagine all the money being wasted but I gave up when I got to "the trillions"

We drove around the Southern tip of Gibraltar and viewed from the sea the southernmost mosque in Western Europe, it is just behind the lighthouse. About as close to Morocco as one can get. I thought I would include this to show that many sailors and oilmen are folk used to a great deal of diversity. Fair enough, just a token, but better than no token at all.

Figure 53 Gibraltar : Lighthouse, Mosque and Rock

We booked a berth in the Ocean Village Marina. According to our pilot book this is the southern of the two marinas within the Ocean Village/Marina Bay marina complex, so I head down there.

"There is a large buoy in the water dead ahead skipper," says the first mate, this is followed by some insistent whistling from the shore, beeping noise from the depth gauge and a rapidly descending depth readout.

"Full reverse thrusters Mr Sulu" shouts the skipper ramming the throttle into full reverse. At that moment a helpful voice comes on the Radio

"You should have the runway on your port side – come down that channel"

"Ah!" says I; "over there" and we proceed more safely than before to our berth, thanking the God's as ever.

It turns out that Ocean Village and Marina Bay marinas merged into one company the year AFTER our pilot book was published and due to extensive renovations, the Ocean Village part was no longer for visiting yachts – however just to confuse everyone – they renamed the whole caboodle "Ocean Village Marina" (even tho' our berth was in what was called the Marina Bay bit) . Ho hum, it does get a bit confusing sometimes.

We had arrived in Gibraltar – 80m away is the runway where Easy Jet and BA run four planes a day between them. Not so bad you think to yourself, but it is also an RAF base, so Tornadoes,Hurricanes and Belfasts also land and take off – and they do not have any reason to keep the noise down. To be fair once darkness had settled we were rarely bothered.

Over the next five days, we do the sights and delights of "Gib". To whit - Tunnels, Apes, Statues, informative Plaques, Red post boxes, Brit style police officers, traffic on the correct side of the road (and this just after we had got used to the opposite, having been in Spain) Jews leaving the Synagogue on a Saturday afternoon, Muslims in Mosque robes on a Friday evening (we didn't see the Christians at all, as they were all socially distancing) but there were Catholic, Anglican, Baptist and Scottish Presbyterian churches available.

This is not the book for "Snaps I took on my holidays" but this one should impress, and as I have a geological bent, it is very dear to my heart.

Figure 54 Limestone caves within the Rock of Gibraltar illuminated by different coloured lights

Figure 55 From Benalmadena to Gibraltar

Chapter 15
Leaving Gibraltar and Orcas

On the following Monday it was off to Barbate. To get the tides right (yes tides; we have now left the Mediterranean and we are officially in the Atlantic) we had to leave at 06:30 in the morning, so it was up early and away. The dawn had not broken yet – so Navigation lights and Radar on. It was quite eerie passing very large ships extremely well illuminated, that were at anchor in the bay. As it became 07:00 hrs the light started to appear in the sky just as we left Algeciras bay, hugging the coast as we had been instructed to do by the pilot book.

The wind started to pick up a bit, so the sails went out and the engine went off and as the dawn rushed in, we were sailing in a healthy breeze almost dead downwind. As we approached Tarifa Point the easterly wind became funnelled (as it does in this area and to be fair, I had been warned) so some discreet 'just a tiny bit too late' reefing was needed.

With 75% main and 80% jib we carried on with eight knots over the ground and one and a half knots of tide under perfect control. It is at this point that my first mate interjects with

"I told you you should have reefed earlier"

Considering her Master's ticket is at the Competent Crew level she has an inherent ability to know when the wind will pick up. Either that or it is just 'worry'.

Our destination that day was Barbate. It has to be admitted that we were very disappointed with Barbate, as it is a soulless remnant of the grandiose plans the local folk had for a smashing sailing hub for the area, that was stymied by the crash of 2008. The marina was mostly empty but very well sheltered – however the town was a good healthy walk away. By the time I visited the town, about two hours after arriving, the wind was blowing a steady thirty knots and sand was blowing everywhere. The beach looked marvellous with golden sand and a lovely promenade with shops and restos everywhere, which I suppose was what encouraged the local Mayor to invest in the Marina. Not an indication of Britishness in sight, in fact very few people spoke English, leaving me to stumble happily in my broken Spanish. It seems the British landed in Gibraltar and only went east to the Costa del Sol and ignored the western part.

It was in Barbate that we met the delivery crew of the Finnish boat *Onnyx*

Figure 56 Onnyx - a rudderless half chewed boat

The boat was a cruiser racer set up for racing and the owner wanted it brought back from Spain to Helsinki. The crew of four comprised a Skipper, Eastern European male in his 50's, two deckies M & F in their late 20.s and a twenty five year old maid called True. They had loaded the boat up with twenty eight day's worth of provisions for four people in Gibraltar and were going to do the trip in one hit. As they left Gibraltar and hit Tarifa point, the thirty knot winds hit them and shredded their Code zero. After they had recovered from that, a pod of Orcas started circling the boat, singing and blowing bubbles under water.

The next thing they knew there was a crash and the Starboard gunwhale was underwater, then another crash and over half the rudder had been bitten off. They knew this because as the boat righted itself, a large piece of laminated foam could be seen floating away followed by another small bit. Both parts with teeth marks in them. Feeling a bit shaken, the Skipper insisted they put their LJ.s on when, the boat was banged about and then turned in a 180 degree circle (Bearing in mind the sails are still out, albeit reefed) For another twenty minutes the Orcas continued to circle, banging the hull and pushing them in different directions. During this phase the skipper puts out a Mayday call, and ensures all crew are wearing their LJ.s and then puts the engine on.

Sails are put away and they try to steer towards shelter – but they cannot keep a course. The skipper tried to steer with the sails, but it was very erratic. Eventually a life boat came and they were offered a tow. It is moments like this when you give great thanks and a contribution to the RNLI as these guys struggled to get a tow on board but eventually the local guys did get a tow together, but in doing so, they smashed the pulpit, but succeeded in towing Onnyx into Barbate.

We met the crew after they had been in port for a week. During this period, four other boats had come in damaged by the Orcas. True reported many white-faced crew entering the port. All the other boats left the next day for repairs in Gibraltar, as they were not so damaged that they could not steer. Unfortunately *Onnyx* could not do so, as the skipper was not happy taking the boat out again. Barbate does not have a big enough crane to get a boat that size out of the water for a visual inspection. It would have to be taken to Gibraltar or Cadiz, both a day's journey away. His insurance would not accept the damage unless there was photographic proof of it, which he could not get and he refused to skipper the boat without a support vessel, as he deemed it too dangerous to proceed. An impasse. Solved by the owner deciding to cancel the contract and coming down to Barbate to take it to Gibraltar himself.

This meant that the skipper and his three crew were free to leave. Thinking what a nice skipper I could be, I offered them a lift to Cadiz where they could get transport to their next jobs or next ports. Only True accepted and so the next day at 10:00 hrs Dofesaba took off to Cadiz with a crew of three. The weather was calm and the wind hovering over eight knots such that the skipper says

"Well why don't we try the 'Bag of Fear?'"

We rarely get this out, but it is a lot safer when there are three on board because if it goes pear shaped, you need a couple of strong folk to manhandle or woman handle the enormous sail into the forepeak. But True was with us and she was a big strong lassie.(and young) So why not.

The wind was still under ten knots and under main and jib we were averaging four knots, the wind was coming from 120-140 deg. off the port quarter, which is ideal for a gennaker. In went the jib and out furled the gennaker. In with the starboard sheet and we were humming along at five and a half knots all very stable and almost perfect.

So perfect, that there was time to note the Point Trafalgar Lighthouse as we passed it, which is a major landmark on the coast. Whereupon my latest crew addition asked

"Why did they name this part of Spain after a square in London"

Figure 57 Point Trafalgar Lighthouse

I explained that 200 years before, this area had been full of fighting square rigged ships, smoke, noise and that men's blood would have coloured the sea red. I explained how Nelson had split the line and defeated the French and Spanish fleets and thereby saved the nation from invasion by Bonaparte, and stopped us all being French, and that it had all happened just about there (he said pointing wildly over the port side). Hence Nelson's column in Trafalgar Square.

"Oh" was all she said.

We stayed like that for nearly two hours until the wind rose to sixteen knots which is my cutoff speed for a very large sail. Nervously I wound the sail in and within five minutes I had wound it tight into a multi coloured rope, all accept one tiny little floppy bit towards the top half of the sail. That didn't matter now, I could sort it out later. Out with the jib, one reef in the main and off we went. The wind maxed out at eighteen knots and unfortunately this persuaded that aforementioned tiny bit of sail to flap annoyingly.

I am told I should have left well alone, but you cannot expect a skipper to try to stop his sails from flogging. Going to the port side I gently tugged on the port sheet, when Whooompf! With a mighty shrill out came half the gennaker.

"Hands to action stations" yelled the skipper (he still doesn't know why, we were not under U-Boat attack) as he tried desperately to wind in the sail. Little did he know but the furling line had been shaken off the furling drum so all his heaving and grunting was useless. Sending True to the front and Mary helping with the furling line and the Port sheet the skipper started the engine and turned the boat into the wind so that when he released the halyard the sail would fall onto the deck and so be under control.

"Mary to the forepeak prepare to receive sail"

Gradually the sail came towards the mast and the mad flapping which had been constant since the above paragraph started, soon abated. The Skipper puts the steering on autopilot and goes to help True on the foredeck. But the wind is too strong.

"True - downstairs help Mary pull the sail in"

This happens, but still it won't come down. Skipper believes it to be well and truly stuck as he can see True, gritting her teeth and heaving like a good'un.

He runs to the mast and winds the halyard in and lo - summat comes unstuck and we can get the sail down. It is bundled down into the forepeak and the lid closed. All three of us meet in the cockpit heaving and sweating. The skipper says

"Well done crew – phew! that was not so much fun"

He turns to the autopilot and resumes course, engine off, then jib out and on we go.

It all took twenty minutes. True says later that she is sailing around the planet getting miles and experiences to help her get her commercial Skippers licence, and that we have helped her by giving her breadth of experience in what CAN happen when using a gennaker – and she will know what to do next time herself.

I felt so pleased.

Figure 58 Muscles Mary and Crew True after we had put the sail away

Chapter 16
CADIZ AND PUERTO SHERRY

We arrived in Cadiz. We chose Puerto America, a marina right at the end of the Cadiz peninsular about as far from Cadiz old town as you can get without getting your feet wet. We berthed and looked out on a massive industrial city port with no saving grace features visible at all.

Further investigation shows that once again, during the noughties, over investment in the infrastructure had occurred, and now what should be boulevards thriving with kiosks and shops, nightclubs and bars is but an empty wasteland. The Club Nautico is the only watering hole this side of a twenty five minute walk into the city, and fortunately it was only five minutes from our berth. As the skipper, I make an executive decision to repair to said Club Nautico and buy the well deserving crew a pint. And so it came to pass.

After saying "farewell and fair winds" to True, who went off on her globe trotting way, we explored Cadiz during the next couple of days but like everything this year, most of the sights were shut, including the wonderful Cathedral. To be fair, a thirty minute walk there and another thirty minute walk back did not endear me to sightseeing particularly in the thirty five degree heat.

After much consideration, we decided to move to Puerto Sherry. Which as its name suggested was a port where Sherry is exported from. At 10:00 hrs we were all ready to go and looking out upwind, all I could see was a massive black cloud coming in. I suggested to Mary that as we were not in any rush, it might be wise to wait "just a wee while" to see what the weather was going to do. The next thing I knew there was an almighty crash and torrential rain descended. Fortunately the Bimini protected us from getting too damp. So we stayed and watched the first storm go over. I poked my head out and blow me down there was another storm lurking just south of the harbour, but this one had lightening within it, so flashing and banging, it too passed over. All the while the boat rocked as the wind whistled through the rigging. Unfortunately I had not turned the instruments on so I could not read the wind speed but it sure felt like more than thirty knots. As that last squall disappeared another smaller storm passed through. By now we were getting quite blasé about wild weather and I was just jolly pleased we had decided not to move from our berth. After another thirty minutes, all had settled down, the sun was out and it dried up all the rain. I expect the spiders came out, it was that sort of day. We cast off and proceeded to Puerto Sherry, in brilliant sunshine with a very slight chop within Cadiz harbour.

Figure 59 The Skipper making sure that the sherry is perfect

When visiting somewhere like Puerto Sherry where you KNOW that there is a local product, it behoves the English visitor to go find out all about it. So I did. I went to the local Bodega; to whit Gutierrez Colosia and found out ALL about how the Spanish produce sherry. They take it very seriously; it is not a drink just for maiden aunts or professors in the 1950's at all. It is a highly refined process entailing patience and skill, and strangely enough we Brits were the ones who invented it back in the 18th Century. While I was there, I saw a brochure for the local Golf Course – so this too had to be visited.

Figure 60   Chipiona Lighthouse, with Mary acting as "Scale"

After two nights it was off to Chipiona . The log says it was a pleasant sail with medium winds and trouble free sailing. We got in at 14:30 and went for lunch. Once again the place was practically deserted and a bit run down. Almost total absence of foreign boats, as if the Spaniards had discouraged everyone from coming. Was it me?

Chipiona is another Spanish holiday town with nice beaches, and very little else. It has a famous lighthouse, which we were encouraged to visit – but as usual it was locked up. It is very difficult to get cultural with all this Virus about. So we didn't.

You can at least see it in the picture, that's Mary down in the Left-hand corner. It is a very grand lighthouse.

Chapter 17
MAZAGON AND EL ROMPIDO

The next stop was Mazagon. Leaving Chipiona, our log says it became very bumpy with erratic winds bang on the nose again. At first this does not sound very comfortable, and it isn't, but it does get a little exciting particularly when the engine is on and the boat is slamming into the rollers. While even a large boat like ours is perfectly safe in those conditions there is a thrill as we hit a big wave, the boat shudders and loses speed and spray comes hurtling over the deck towards the helmsman, ensuring he ducks under the sprayhood to avoid a face full.

The crew, who is dutifully looking out of the starboard window and around the starboard side of the sprayhood, also ducks inside too. It is in conditions like this that one can easily trap a lobster pot or other trailing lines. (This coast is notorious for tuna netting) bearing in mind we have TWO rudders, albeit each one is shorter than most, so we have to be doubly careful. After several hours of this I contemplate putting the sails out, but I am reminded what happens every time I think this way by she who knows better. And lo it came to pass within fifteen minutes the wind has risen to twenty knots gusting twenty five knots, still bang on the nose and I decide that putting the sails out was not such a good idea after all and why did I even think it would be allowed, being only the mere skipper.

So we get to Mazagon, surely one of the most boring places on the coast. Nothing except beaches either side and as the weather was not that good, there were very few visitors and very few families enjoying the delights of said beaches. The marina was sparsely populated and appeared run down with almost no-one there. Only one bar, and that was boring too. No sights to see, but as it was Washing Day we had to stay for two nights.

A small diversion on Washing.

While we don't wear very many clothes while in Spain/Portugal, We do get through several T shirts and shorts per week. It is very warm in these parts Also our bedding gets "used", what with sun tan oil and general human sweat, sheets can become a bit "soiled" (I hope you notice how discreet and sensitive

I am being here). So the Bosun er... who is also the crew, has wisely decided that to prevent nits, crabs, lice and other critters living in our bedding, it has to be washed at least once a week. It also has to have a minimum of four hours drying in sunshine.

Fortunately, we have a small washing machine on board that can take a sheet at a time (I know – call ourselves real sailors) so for most of a day we will do three to five washes of about one and a half hours each. Can you imagine doing this in Laundromats, particularly in some of the marinas we have visited, where there is a thirty minute walk to the nearest town or where we find the marina washing and drying machines arebroken. Then there is getting the required change. All very well, but in Covid times there just aren't the people or the open shops or bars to go get change from. Now you know why we are so pleased with our little washing machine. All the drying is done by God, and rarely takes long.

Our next destination was El Rompido where we had a booked berth. Now El Rompido is a bit special. It has been an old fishing harbour for centuries and a holiday town since the 1960's. Its saving grace is that it is fully protected by a large sand spit called 'The Arrow of Rompido' that forms the South bank of the river as it empties seven km to the East. And there is the rub, because where it empties into the sea is a sand bar, and that sand bar, like all good sand bars, has a mind of its own. It changes height and position on a regular basis. One is advised to exercise extreme caution when entering or leaving the river. Our pilot book advised us to start well outside the entrance and come in orthogonal to the coast, but we, being more adventurous and having a lifting keel decided we would go for the short cut.

Figure 61 The Entrance to El Rompido

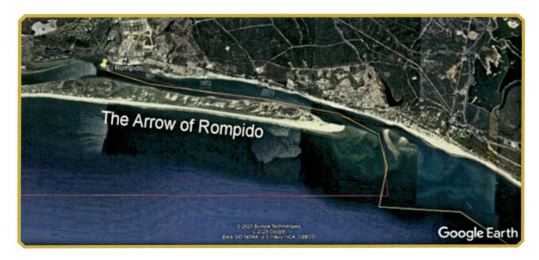

However it was still necessary to identify the port and starboard marker buoys as well as the Fairway Buoy. (For non-cruisers, the Fairway Buoy is a distinctive colour, it looks like Signal toothpaste, having red and white vertical stripes. and marks the start of your expected run in. The safe track starts there and is marked by the red and green marker buoys, these show the edges of the safe channel)

As we approached, I could see several green and red buoys and also a big yellow thing in the water – but no Fairway Buoy. This was a little disconcerting as the depth was decreasing smoothly but steadily, and finding the start of the safe channel was necessary for me to know where to sneak into said channel. Still puzzled, we gradually got closer and closer. Suddenly, there was a big splash at the stern of the yellow thing (bearing in mind I am using binoculars constantly here) and a Fairway Buoy magically appears. All is well, and we continue on our way safely.

I found out later from the Capitainerie in halting English and Spanish – that this was the week all the channel buoys were being re-positioned and the Fairway Buoy was the last to be done. The big yellow thing, was the vessel specially designed to pick up the buoys and their accompanying massive concrete block anchors and move them into the new positions.

"Well" says I "what a nice thing to do for us visiting yachtsmen"

"Oh don't you worry it is not for you, it is for the fishermen" says the Capitaine, properly putting me in my place. Whatever; it allowed us to get safely into our berth.

El Rompido was a pleasant town, which at one point had been a place for the British to Holiday, but all the English bars had been taken over by Spaniards and there were very few obvious remains of the British Holiday way of life. Except for a super Golf course that had to be played. Unlike many ports we had visited there was no evidence of over investment and the place hummed with Spanish families and consequently all the shops and bars were open. We had a lovely time there.

The day before we had planned to leave, a British boat called *Dolphin* entered our marina and parked right next door to us. Being the sociable sailors we are, we invited them for a few sherbets on the back deck. They were pleasant company but could not stay long as they were catching the first tide and leaving at 06:00 the following day, so off they went to bed early to get a good night's sleep. We went out for dinner and retired to bed around 23:00.

I was rudely awoken at 06;15 with a massive bang that shook the whole boat. I won't write what I said, but I leapt out of bed and tried to climb the companion way.

"I think you should put some shorts on first dear" said the First Mate.

She had a point. So in shorts and nowt else I ran upstairs to find *Dolphin* impaled on our bowsprit with her skipper vainly holding her off. At the rear was the Helmsman/Crew vainly holding the rear of their boat off the bowsprit off the boat next door. They were pinned by the tide and every time they tried to get away, the tide pushed them back on to the bowsprits, so they were getting nowhere. We rushed up to help (By this time Mary had come up with a torch, looking very elegant in her kimono) and I managed to keep them off while the skipper ran back to help the helmsman. After ten minutes of hot sweaty work, they managed to extricate themselves and with a less than cheery "We will call you in the morning and pay for any damage" they were gone and we retired to our bed. Hours later I went forwards and checked – not a scratch, which cheered us both up, as *Dolphin* had lost at least two stanchions and sustained some other minor damage.

We left Rompido as early as we could, but that still meant after 15:30 hrs giving us five hours to get to our next destination before darkness. We were off to the Isla Christina.

Figure 62 Gibraltar to Isla Christina

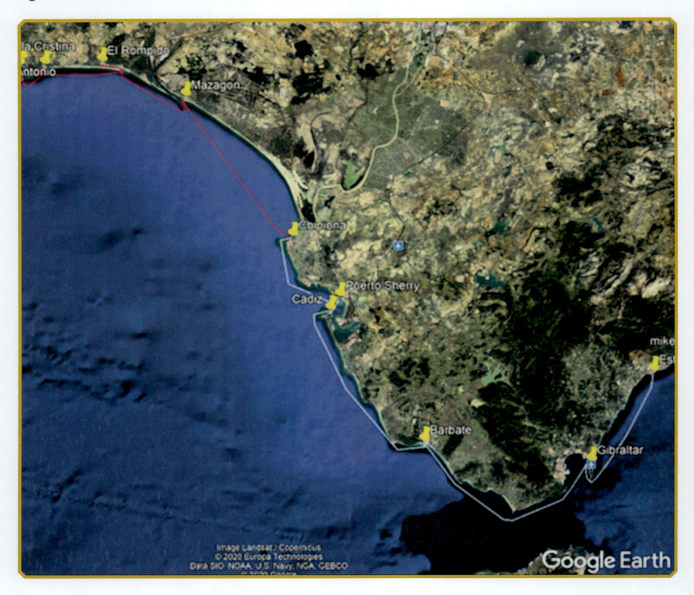

Chapter 18
To Isla Christina and Ayamonte

As we left El Rompido for the seven Km journey to the tricky entrance (now the exit) we passed many pleasure boats scootling about, towing parasails, water skis, inflated hoops with screaming children on and many Spanish holiday makers enjoying water sports and the beaches. We were right in the middle of the main Mediterranean holiday month of August, and the place was quite crowded. Once again I noticed that even tho' it was crowded there weren't any disputes or people attacking anyone else or children behaving badly, and I had seen many adults getting into the wine and spirits with their morning coffee, and this year, when they were supposed to, EVERYONE wore their Masquarilla at the appropriate time and place.

Our journey took us past many lobster pots, some we saw far away and some we saw just in time, but not one did we catch; thank heavens.

We arrived at Isla Cristina Marina and got into our berth and as it was quite late, we dined on board ready to explore the following day. Isla Cristina has a large fishing quay and processing plants behind it. It is one of the foremost fishing ports in Spain. To the south is the beach and tourist parts populated mainly by the people of Sevilla who come for the beaches and the clean water. (and probably the fish). It is another of those towns where over investment has occurred in anticipation of a massive upturn in the marine market. It seems that every town along the coast expected every holiday maker to invest in an expensive boat that would be stored in THEIR marina/town and not any one else's. If only there had been a centralised hand on the tiller of the local State, competent enough to guide each individual mayor.

Isla Cristina had invested in some massive sheds which were designed to store RIBs and small boats. The sheds were up to five stories high; giving a capacity for several thousand boats. Obviously these did not arrive and the marina was left with these storage areas looking very forlorn and almost totally empty

Figure 63 vertical boat shed storage. All empty

As we had seen enough beaches and dereliction, Mary and I were not that enamoured and left for Ayamonte after two nights.

It is not a long way to Ayamonte when you look at the **map**. However when you look at the **chart** you realise that there is an enormous bank of sand that has been brought down the River Guadiana and dumped right in the way of an easy passage from Isla Catarina, causing a major diversion towards the ocean. We tried to cut across this but even with our lifting keel, the depth was too shallow, and round the outside we had to go.

The River Guadiana is the border between Spain and Portugal and has been for centuries. They seem to manage it very well and to be fair it was never an issue all the time we were on it. Safely, we entered Ayamonte marina.

Ayamonte is a pleasant town and one of the few we entered with real live "foreign tourists" in it. I don't know if they had come over from Portugal or what, but it was one of the most thronged towns we visited. Mind you, it was not so difficult for there to be a thronging, as many of the streets were very narrow as befits a medieval town. Most of the port area was pedestrianised, and mainly designed now for the foreign tourist. I tried to get some Culture but all the churches and the one museum were closed. I nearly got accepted into a convent, thinking it looked like an interesting church and managed to get a little way in, until a small round nun suggested very politely that this was a closed order and I was not welcome – I left hurriedly and decided not to make a habit of it (Boom Boom).

Figure 64 Little Gems in the Plaza

The town was full of the usual restos, Cafes and plazas, which included many statues and wall pictures and street furniture decorated with colourful locally made tiles. This just had to do to fulfil my need for exciting things to see. Large parts of the hinterland remain unfinished development, but at least one Golf Course was completed so I decided to avail myself. I paid my fee and was told that I would have to partner someone, as singles were not allowed out in the summer.

Arriving at the first tee I spied a mature gentlemen and what was obviously his grandson, being a slight child/youth, called Jorge – but only one set of clubs. I duly introduced myself in halting Spanish and they replied that they had no English, but I was here to play golf – so.

They offered me the opportunity to tee off first, which is always nerve wracking but my first shot was not bad – a good solid start, sighs of relief. The Grandfather selected his driver then gave it to Jorge who teed himself up, looked down the course, walked away, squinted down towards the hole, teed himself up again, wiggled his butt, looked up, drew back his driver and smacked the ball well past mine. With a satisfied nod he marched off down the course leaving his grandfather to bring his clubs. To say I was amazed is an understatement – it continued for the next 9 holes in exactly the same manner, except I was able to outdrive him – once. On every shot he performed his ritual like the true professional golfer he was obviously destined to be. It turned out that Jorge was ten years old and had been playing since he was four, and was the local Junior state champion. A large wind would have blown him over. I am more traditionally built (as Mma Ramotswe would say, not quite that traditionally built, but I am no slim jim) I am also 65 years old and play off twenty one. He was ten, half my height and weighed nothing. I beat him by one shot on handicap (Grandad was scorer) I did not feel a great sense of victory, but he smiled when he said goodbye and I wished him well. I only hope he does not lose interest when he reaches adolescence, otherwise I am certain I shall be seeing a lot more of him on TV.

Figure 65 State Junior Champion Jorge and Grandfather

Chapter 19
LEAVING SPAIN

The following day it was off to Puerto Santo Antonio. A massive journey (See map below) across the River Guadiana to the Portuguese side to be ready to pick up our two new crew, who had flown out of the UK and were due there at 17:00.

Now Puerto San Antonio was a river marina, just like East Cowes on the Isle of Wight. In that the river flows through the pontoons and this can run at around three knots on a bad day. I had taken some local advice as to when to leave and so I arrived there just as the tide turned, and the flow was at a minimum. Just at that moment the VHF called us.

Figure 66 The entrance to the Rio Guardiana

"Dofesaba II please do not enter the Marina yet, as we do not have a berth for you"

I was a bit surprised at this, as when I had called earlier in the day, they assured me there was space, so I agreed and went on a series of circles just outside the harbour entrance. I suppose it must have looked a bit strange to onlookers, as what was this skipper doing, he doesn't seem to know the way in.

Eventually after half an hour, I got the all clear to proceed and so I was a bit miffed to find the water moving through the pontoons when I got near to the entrance – again. Now the entrance is very narrow and channels within the Marina are very tight. There is a vicious right turn as soon as you enter the marina to get "up the channels between the pontoons". However as we turned right, Mary spotted two Marineros (or whatever the Portuguese version is called because we were now in Portugal and consequently an hour behind where we were the other side of the river where we started)

"They want us to berth there" says she, and right she was. There was a tiny half a hammerhead sticking out the front of a large yacht that appeared unoccupied, and I was already nearly past it. Once again the cry went down to the engine room.

"Full Reverse thrusters Mr Sulu – now" as I gently but firmly put the prop into 'Backwards'. A fourteen ton boat does not stop immediately no matter how fast the propellor turns and we continued to glide past our berth, albeit slowing steadily, until we had lost all way and direction. The tide was also pushing us closer and closer to the next set of berths on the pontoon after our hammerhead. Some very sweaty moments passed before I had full control of the boat whereby I turned Dofesaba II with bow thruster support, to point back the way we had come and into the current. Then it was relatively easy to come up to where the two marineros were standing and gradually slide a 12.5m boat into a 7.5m berth. (Obviously with five metres sticking out into the marina – which is not ideal). We could not be any further from the pedestrian exit if we had tried. The marineros left and we tidied up and then set out to find our new crew.

We were lucky that Terry and Siobhan were smart enough to follow our instructions, as within fifteen minutes of entering a Café we saw them turn up by Taxi and walk into said Café.

A small diversion on Crewing services.

Many organisations (The Royal Yachting Association, The Cruising Association, and most yacht clubs) run a system online where those Cruisers who need Crew and those Crews who do not have a boat but want to increase their miles, or even those who just like cruising different places; can be put together. The Skipper asks for the type of Crew he wants, specifies certain things (like - no smokers, no pets, no single men for instance) describes the boat, specifies planned destinations and timings and then sits back and waits for offers. The Crews browse all the offerings and contact the chosen Skipper through the site and ask if they are suitable. In normal times crew and skipper would meet for dinner or lunch and ensure they were at least on the same hymn sheet. During the Covid year, we had a quick Zoom call, and that was that, so we had never met them in the flesh until the Café. Fortunately it was just fine and it all worked really well, and they were a pleasure to have on board.

We returned to the boat, showed them around and asked what they would like to do. We ended up planning to go up the River Guadiana the following morning to a place called Alcoutim. There was only one small problem. The bridge above Ayamonte. (see Figure 66 at the top of the picture)

All skippers should know the dimensions of their boat, and all should be aware of the tidal range in the area they are sailing. With this knowledge one can navigate under bridges (Going over them is for cars & lorries.)

A Small diversion on getting under Bridges

When Dofesaba II was built, the top of the mast was 18.73 m above the waterline. But after that, one has to put on a top light which contains the anchor light and tri-colour nav lights. This brought the height to 19m. Then I have two VHF aerials about a metre long which gives me an airdraft of 20m A nice easy number to remember.

The airdraft of the Bridge was specified on the chart as 18m. Now in UK that is the lowest it could ever be as it is measured from the Highest Astronomical Tide (HAT) so all you have to do is wait for the tide to drop 2.5m and I would pass under safely. BUT the Spanish are clever. They measure bridge heights from Mean Sea Level, which in this area is about 1.0m below HAT so I would need nearly 3.5m of tide drop to get under safely, and the tide only dropped three metres. I was missing half a metre. It seemed impossible.

I explained all this to Terry & Siobhan and they just looked disappointed and we cannot have that. On Dofesaba II we do not use the word "impossible" nor "ooooh we'd better not", where is the adventure in that we ask? What they did not know was that I had spoken to a British charter boat skipper berthed next door to us in Ayamonte and asked him about this. He had the same mast as me on a Bavaria 41 and he just said -

"If you can see one metre of mud on the banks either side and stay in the middle – you'll be right, I have done it hundreds of times over the last 13 years" This is referred to as 'Local Knowledge'.

Well what could possibly go wrong with that advice. We set off at half tide and as we got to the bridge after half an hour I could see one metre of mud. As a precaution I slowed right down stemming the ebbing tide so we crawled under the bridge at about 0.3 knots in a place where the bed supports of the road weren't and slipped gradually under; safely.

"Phew I thought we would touch there" I heard all around me. Going under a bridge always looks closer than it really is and I reckoned we had a metre and a half to spare from the top of the aerials – but it was still a heart in the mouth moment.

We pootled up the Guadiana following the well marked channel as it twisted and turned as rivers do.

We passed many farms and homesteads on the Portugese side and just fields and woods on the Spanish side, it was all very lovely and peaceful in the hot Mediterranean sun.

Eventually we got to Alcoutim where we were promised several pontoons to berth against. I saw a lovely space and made as if to land. This caused all sorts of arm waving and shouting by several "local " looking chaps, which obviously I did not fully understand but I got the general drift,

"err... you can't park that there yacht 'ere mate" – which they would have said if they came from South London – which they didn't.

I aborted our run in, as I tried to think and find somewhere else to park. While I was circling the boat, I noticed two old boys fiddling with the warps on a small boat already parked on the pontoon. After some minutes I noticed a small gap had suddenly become a bigger gap.

"Can you get in here?" asked a voice in English.

"I'll give it a damn good try" says I. Well I didn't have any choice – there wasn't anywhere else to go and they had been very nice shifting their boat up to make room.

I prepared the crew and told them it would be a tight fit and a bit stressy but the chaps on the pontoon looked like they could deal with a rope if needed. And so it turned out to be, I turned up into the flow, came alongside the rearmost yacht so my stern was just past level with the bow and gently ferry glided sideways into the space. My bowsprit went over the bowsprit of the boat at the front – that's how tight it was, lines were thrown and were tied down. We had managed to get a 12.9m yacht into a 13.5m space without hitting anything. This pleased all on the pontoon who owned the boat in the front and looking up, I saw several Portuguese villagers smiling and nodding. After such a success we settled down for a refreshingly cold beer on the back deck, knowing we were safe and secure until at least tomorrow.

Figure 67 The longest aerial runway in Europe

As I looked out northwards, beer in hand, I saw a person floating past at speed, but 50 metres up in the air. He/she disappeared behind a tree at a prodigious rate. I looked at the beer can – it was only 4.2%, I thought hard –yes it was my first one of the day.

"Did anyone else see that?"

"See what?"

"A person flying through the air – over there" I pointed northwards and just at that moment, another one came over. It was an aerial runway, which started from the top of a hill in Spain to a river valley about 50m above river level in Portugal. When you looked very carefully one could see a cabin on the hill in Spain and binoculars showed a queue of people in Spain waiting to hurtle to their imminent deaths in Portugal. (I wonder who would have responsibility if there were accidents) Apparently it is the longest Aerial Runway in Europe and very famous in the under 35 year age group. I had never heard of it. We took a collective crew decision that it was not for us and trying out the local restaurants was a better bet.

While we were sitting there by the Pontoon, one of the old boys said

"Well it was a good idea you did not go past the end of the pontoon because, you see that river there, (which was where the Aerial Runway disappeared into) that there river empties out just here and deposits loads of sand and rock, 50m beyond the Pontoon, which is why the port hand marker is there"

Well I had noticed the PHM as we were circling around and had very nearly bashed into it, going so close that we missed it by a metre. (Which is WAY too close but at least we missed it). And a good job I had been that close too as further away I would have hit the sandbar/rocky outcrop. I think it was on our second beer that we noticed another small yacht come upriver obviously looking for a berth on the Portuguese side. He was mid stream as he went past us and then he went further upstream. Just as I was about to turn away he turned sharply to port and came straight towards us. His line was well inside the PHM post, which he avoided very well, far better than I did.

I turned to Terry

"I think he is coming in to raft up next to us, I think we should get fenders ready" This is Skipper speak for -

"I think YOU should get fenders ready" we both stood up and then we both looked a bit puzzled.

"He is taking it very cautiously" I said

"Maybe the incoming tide is still fierce", I looked down at the water which was actually going out pretty rapidly by now.

"No! I think he is stuck on the sand bar" and so it turned out to be.

Figure 68 It's all happening in Alcoutim

This poor couple had snagged the sand and they could not move, and we could not help them either. The local ferry (flat bottomed with a large outboard engine) went over to check they were OK, which they were, and they decided to stay on the boat. Every hour we checked on them until dark. As time passed, the boat heeled further and further over until the port gunwhale was well and truly underwater and they were struggling to stand upright.

At about 0100 hrs Terry and Siobhan were awakened by cries of activity and jubilation. Seems like they got off and sailed away to a better anchorage, bowed but unharmed.

The next day we sloped off to do some sightseeing, examining the local Fort (small 17th-18th Century – not much to see except a few standard cannon), when we heard of a place to go swimming in clear river water. Siobhan was keen and we had no objections as, where there is swimming there is generally a Café. We found it up the river past where the Aerial Runway end was stationed. In a meander of the river one km. from the town, some enterprising person had built a beach, including beach bar. If you are Spanish and love the beach concept, as almost all Spaniards will admit to, and you live miles from the sea and you cannot afford a holiday cottage somewhere else, you get the Mayor to bring sand from the coast and build a beach on your doorstep. And so he did. I bet he gets re-elected every year. We all enjoyed the totally unexpected facilities and thanked him very much.

Figure 69 Alcoutim River Beach (and Bar)

Leaving Alcoutim was not so difficult, but we had to be careful not to arrive at the Bridge too early. Once again, I aimed for half tide falling, having calculated that this would occur at 17:30 hrs at the bridge. However everyone knows that judging tidal heights in flowing rivers is always tricky as so many factors influence how much water is actually there.

We must have left too early because I crawled the last five miles and still we arrived with too much water. By now the river was running at two knots towards the sea so there was very little I could do anyway. As we approached the bridge, I managed to convince myself that on the upstream side I could see one metre of mud. With confidence I steered for the same highest point of the Bridge as we skimmed underneath at about 2.5 knots. There was a communal sucking in of breath as we made it by about 30 centimetres, I mean it was VERY close. We all looked at each other as if to say "That was a bit too close for comfort", but we had made it. On the downstream side of the bridge there was very little mud visible on the banks. We pulled into Ayamonte for a debrief.

I have thought long and hard about that last bit, how did we get away with it?. Here are several possible reasons why:

When measured on dry land the height of the mast top plus aerials is 20m above the designed waterline. But we had a full boat with water, fuel, people, baggage, bikes, washing machines and other stuff. This must make us sit down a bit deeper.

The river is mainly non-salt water, this gives us less buoyancy than sea water and contributes a bit more to less height.

The Bridge height is measured from the lowest point that could impact anything going under it. We transited at the highest point which probably saved a metre at least.

It was mid-summer, there would have been less water coming down from the hills.

Wikipedia says the "Maximum Height above the water" is 20m. not 18m.

The Lord shines upon the righteous; and poor sailors.

Chapter 20
LEAVING SPAIN - AGAIN

The next day dawned bright and calm. As we left the safety of the river the wind peaked at ten knots dead on the stern. I turned to Terry

Figure 70 Peter's Parasailor in Portugal

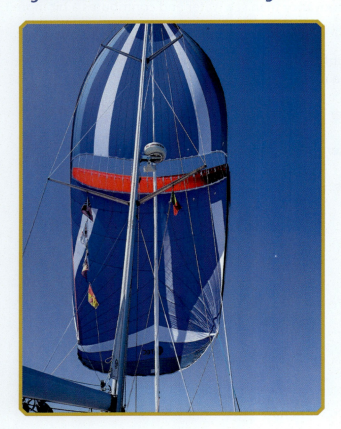

"Have you ever sailed a Parasailor?" followed by "Would you like to?" Good old Terry, he was up for it, and the conditions were ideal.

A small diversion on downwind sails, as carried on Dofesaba II

You know we carry a gennaker, (see Chapter 13). Termed the 'Bag of fear' because EVERY time we get it out something goes wrong. Now a Parasailor is very different from a gennaker. A gennaker attaches to the Bowsprit, the top of the mast and to a sheet that controls how open and closed it is. There is one sheet per side (That's two then, one green and one red) You can fly a gennaker from +-110 to +-160 deg.s to the direction of the boat. Note the missing +-20 deg.s (160 – 180) gennakers do not like dead down wind. However Parasailers do. They are basically a Spinnaker with a wing in the middle, and they require two sheets and two guys and a headsail rope. I have flown them from +-85 deg to 180 deg. They get a bit dangerous in winds over twenty knots and they require at least three people on board to set and control properly, which is why Mary and I rarely use it. They are also quite expensive which is why few sailors have them.

I explained to the crew what we were going to do and went forward to start fixing the ropes to the various parts of the sail on the foredeck. When all was ready Terry hoisted the sausage of sail up to the top of the mast and when we were all ready, I pulled hard on the snuffer line. The wind caught the sail and with a small whirr this massive beautiful blue sail blossomed in front of me. I trimmed the controls and settled back into the cockpit – and there we were, doing five knots in an eight knot wind with the wind dead behind, and the Parasailer was as steady as a rock. Of course I tried to improve on this, but every time I trimmed a sheet or pulled in a guy, we slowed down or lost shape. I was eventually prevailed upon to leave well alone.

We stayed like this for three hours until the wind decreased to five knots and the sail collapsed. Getting it down was easy, pull on the snuffing line (Which turns a massive sail into an easily manipulated sausage of compressed ripstop) pack it down the forehatch and then on with the iron topsail to get us to our destination, while Terry and I went downstairs and stuffed the Parasailer into its bag and stowed it away until next time.

We had been told by the Charter skipper in Ayamonte that the Isla Culatra was not to be missed. It was "authentic" (he was younger than us) very safe, and a different experience. It was to be our next destination.

Chapter 21
Isla Culatra - Vilamoura

The anchorage at Isla Culatra has two entrances. Both can be seen in Figure 71. At first glance the Eastern entrance on Google Earth looks very viable, particularly in a lifting keel yacht. The Pilot book suggests that any skipper attempting this passage would be wise to get local knowledge first. Well, being adventurous as you may have gathered we are, some would say unfairly 'on the cusp of foolhardy', the gallant ship Dofesaba II gradually approached the eastern entrance. About one Mile (nautical) away, scanning ahead with binoculars, all I could see was an unbroken line of breaking white water. This tended to suggest that the sand bar had fully closed the "entrance" and discretion should win over superfluous valour. Sighing quietly, I turned to port and towards the Westerly entrance while the crew breathed sighs of relief.

Figure 71 Isla Culatra anchorage; the village is by the pin.

We motored gradually up stream towards the anchorage and there it was. About thirty yachts all swinging happily on their moorings. Apparently, this anchorage takes over a hundred visitors in normal years but once again Covid had struck. We did not see any foreign yachts at all. After checking and re-checking the anchor, we dinghied into the port, a matter of 2-300 metres and "landed". The port was particularly unwelcoming allowing only dinghies inside, and then only in the most inconvenient place. We disembarked and wandered about the village. I don't know what it is about people who live on secluded islands, they tend to be; well insular, close knit, suspicious (not particularly friendly) towards strangers and generally a bit weird. The small sample we took on our three hour visit to Isla Culatra demonstrated this in spades. Not only that, but no-one wished to keep their bar/resto open after dark as this would encourage people to miss the last passenger ferry back to the mainland and so the visitors would have to stay overnight. As dusk became imminent, we re-embarked into the dinghy and returned to Dofesaba II and dined like kings on board.

The forecast the following day was winds behind us twelve to sixteen knots. Terry suggested that he would really like to try the Parasailer again.

My experiences with forecasts in Spain had shown there was a certain erratic-ness within the system. Normally twelve to sixteen becomes twenty knots as soon as I put any sail out. With the Parasailer there was no reefing, it was all or nothing and it is a big powerful sail and as we only had a three hour trip I thought it would not be worth it. I told a disappointed Terry that I was not sure it was such a good idea and we would not be playing with the Parasailer. I even explained my reasoning. He took it well and did not grump in any way; well not that I heard anyway.

So for three hours we had a lovely gentle sail on full main and jib and the wind speed indicator never went north of twelve knots. He didn't say a word, which was very sporting of him. We arrived in Villamoura totally unstressed, and sometimes that can be a good thing, with this, I consoled myself.

Vilamoura is one of those marinas that belong East of Malaga in Spain. It is almost totally British. There were several curry houses (which the Spanish hate) as well as five Irish bars, and Fish'n Chips in most Bars. Strangely enough there were many Brits holidaying in the local hotels, but there were very few if any boats in the marina with the red duster.

Terry and Siobhan were not too impressed, and were not keen on staying another day, but I had heard that locally there was a whole Roman town that had recently been unearthed, and as I had been suffering from a complete dearth of Roman ruins, and to be fair any kind of ruin, museum, church or any cultural artefact for the whole summer – I just had to go and see them.

Figure 72 The Roman remains showing the paths of the old silted up rivers

Bare in mind that last year I had done nothing but visit so many Roman and Moorish artefacts (I even make an exception for 16th Century Palaces and Castles) and this year I think I had seen one church so far. (see 'The Adventures of Dofesaba II 2019 – The Punic Coast' or Chapters 1-11 of this book) The site was within 500 m. of the marina – so off I strolled all alone early one morning hoping for a good days sightseeing.

The Museum was closed – Covid, but one was allowed to wander about. The settlement was very tiny, no more than a Roman Villa on a stream where a few local fishing boats had probably been based. There was a small house (for Romans) with mosaics and bath houses and several temples but nothing grand. There were examples of fish processing for that weird Roman fish sauce called Garum that they all seemed to enjoy, as well as wine storage. It was obvious that the Roman settlement had declined after the Visigoths had invaded, as this port was not big enough or wealthy enough to support a social structure that was not as rigid as that supporting a Roman magistrate within the late Roman Empire.

The town had then blossomed when the Moors invaded, and the Moors being jolly clever had "improved" the Roman baths, as they did in Sevilla and generally tidied things up for a few hundred years until once again it went into decline following the re-conquering by the Catholic Monarchs Ferdinand and Isabella, who drove the last of the Moors out of Spain.

After that, the village descended into nothingness until the 20th Century. Then the river port was blocked up with the coming of the Marina and holiday homes in the 1960's. It was renamed Vilamoura – or the Town of the Moors, because at that time most of the Roman influence had been subsumed and the Roman influence was only found with more modern archaeological techniques. But you can't call all towns Vila Romanum or no-one would know where they were. So Vilamoura it remained.

Chapter 22
THE FINAL STRETCH

Saying goodbye to Guinness and Fish'n Chips we headed out to sea, off to visit Portimao, one of the sardine capitals of the world. We made a strategic decision NOT to go into Albufeira as most of us had had enough of ersatz holiday entertainment of the British overseas kind. To be fair the Marina looked quite good from far out to sea – so we all agreed to leave it at that. I refer to one of the first paragraphs of this narrative regarding the Skippers ability to make hard and fast decisions regarding routing and timing.

The wind was under four knots and from the wrong direction, so it was on with the engine, as can happen in this area at this time of year. On our way we passed so many twenty man ribs carrying holiday makers out to see the cliffs that I was prevailed upon to take Dofesaba II further inland to see what all the excitement was about. Fortunately the cliffs are on a sunken coast and in the main the sea bottom descended almost vertically from the cliff base and we were able to get safely within thirty metres of the cliffs. These cliffs were composed of a soft honey coloured limestone that had been weathered by the sea into arches, stacks and caves, interspersed with rias and beaches. The tourists were being shown the main big caves that they could drive into. With a twenty metre air draft I could not get into any of the caves or duck under any of the arches but it was jolly pleasant to look at all the geological formations.

Figure 73 Limestone cliffs at sea level

After about twenty minutes of gliding along the coast, dodging the shore and loads of buzzy mega powered ribs, it all got a bit samey. So we decided to carry on our way and hove off to Portimao.

Portimao is a big marina with some big boats in it. It has a subtle look of neglect, nowhere near as much as the other places before mentioned, but not full and not thriving. There were very few shops and Cafes inside the marina and just outside there were some beach kiosks. Then we wandered to the actual beach on the South side of the Marina and Hotel complex. What a difference, about twenty bars and restos including shops and beach shops. Sadly underpopulated but at least they were open. We hove off to a beach club that our membership of the Marina allowed us into. It had hot and cold running waiters and waitresses, and a large pool. We were all dying for a swim, particularly Siobhan who had been missing her daily dip.

When I asked where we could change into our swimming costumes the reply was a little startling.

"I am sorry Senor, but you are not allowed to use the Pool. You can buy our very expensive coffee and beer, and it will be brought to your table by our very attractive waitresses, but you cannot use the 'oh so inviting' pool you see before you".

Well we were obviously very disappointed, but not surprised. It is something that Mary & I had encountered all along the coast of Spain. Our Pilot book, which was not too out-of-date had promised cool inviting pools of clear water in Marina Clubs all along the coast from the Costa Brava all the way to the Algarve – yet whenever we tried to enter or use the pool, it was for Members only, and not for 'poor bloody sailors'. I have no idea whether this was a Covid thing, but I suspect not, as it happened last year too. I had asked in Spain and been told it was a new policy, but no-one had an answer as to why the policy had changed.

We decided not to be churlish and start a fight, so we gently finished our drinks and went elsewhere.

The following day it was time for an adventure. Terry and Siobhan were keen to try out the Torqueedo electric motor again, and find out its capabilities, so we decided to dinghy across the River Arade to Ferragudo, being on the other bank of the fast flowing river. It was a lovely sunny day with a gentle wind and both the tide and wind was with us as we gently motored across to the quay in Ferragudo which was about one km. away.

Figure 74 Our dinghy trip

Ferragudo is really where the sardines come from, as there is still a large fishing harbour there. Apparently, the sardine canning factories were in Portimao along with all the wealthy owners and their houses, so all the workers, who lived in Ferragudo, had to row across the river in all weathers to go to work. The workforce was most likely to be the wives and daughters of the fishermen, who lived near to the port in Ferragudo. Since the millennium, all the factories except one have been demolished and wealthy holiday homes built in their place. Such is the world we inhabit. 'Come the revolution brothers', as they say.

Ferragudo is very picturesque, with narrow streets and lots of family run bars and sardineries. We found a lovely one in the square and really enjoyed ourselves, getting stuffed with sardines and well lubricated for very little expense. We liked Portugal.

When we returned to the Quay, we found that the tide had come in and was starting to go out again (I call that planning) so our dinghy was only just below the level of the Quay top. This is good for getting unsteady people into small six man dinghies, particularly when having to go down steps covered in algae or to give it the more popular name "Slime". However it is not so good when the wind has increased from "gentle" to "fresh". As soon as we pushed off from the quay, I realised that we now had wind against tide and every half-second we were hitting waves that threw spray up into the air. Mary and Siobhan were not having a good time, being right at the front. Terry and I were sheltered behind them so it was not too bad for us. Being a considerate skipper and wishing to keep my marriage together and my crew happy, I altered course to mitigate the spray, but this made us roll alarmingly and took us away from our destination. As you know there is always a Doris Stokes solution, which I found (eventually). Tired and a little damp we returned to the boat.

We had used up 35% of our battery power, so answering Terry's question. We had travelled just under two km. in distance. These sorts of things are important to know.

We couldn't keep on eating sardines, so the next day it was off to Lagos, our final station stop as they say irritatingly on South-West trains. (It is either a station or a stop, you do not need both, an acceptable alternative is "Destination") Lagos has a good reputation as an overwintering harbour and the local boatyard Sopromar is well considered by the British boating community for doing a good job. This was reassuring as I had booked a nine month berth for the boat for the winter. Which is all a skipper needs. I would not say they were cheap – but reasonable is good.

We had arrived several days earlier than expected, so we did the washing and sorted the boat out as best we could, even a little sightseeing, but once again I thoroughly failed to find an open church, and Lagos has many. Apparently, the town was founded by the Romans and was the home of Henry the Navigator, as well as Portugal's capital city. Well now it is home to Dofesaba II until May next year; hopefully.

We had to say a sad farewell to Terry and Siobhan. We had enjoyed their company and they had been a very welcome addition to the crew indeed. I am convinced that without their help we would not have been so adventurous, and we had enjoyed some lovely evenings together. After ten days within a boat, not one cross word was heard.

Figure 75 The Crew – Terry, Siobhan and Mary

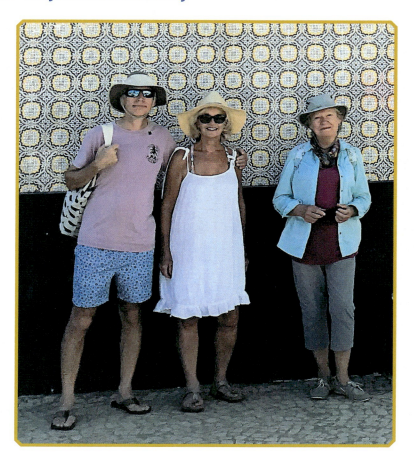

Mary and I stayed on for another five days awaiting our flight and gradually sorting out work to be done and by whom. Including getting the sprayhood and cockpit tent to a local sailmaker for urgent repairs.

Figure 76 Happily nestled in Lagos Marina awaiting our return in May 2021(?)

A small diversion on Sunshine in the Med.

As I have said before, it gets pretty hot out in the Mediterranean Sea, as well as further inland (Where Europe's only official desert lives – See The Adventures of Dofesaba II 2019 or Chapter 10). I don't think we British sailors who leave our boats in the Med appreciate how hot it can get from March to May and Sept to November, if only on odd days.

There is also the rain that carries sandy particles blown into the lower atmosphere from the sand sea in the Sahara (way south of the Atlas mountains in Morocco, Algeria and Tunisia) These particles are carried on a Southerly wind to dump over southern Spain. Last year the rain dumped the grit onto our windows and then the sun came up and melted the plastic windows so embedding the grit within the windows. This meant that for the whole summer we could hardly see through them. This is not good when travelling along the track of a lobster pot boat. Rule one : Take ALL the canvas off the poles for the winter, including the Spray hood. Mind you, we did take the Cockpit tent down and stored it, and when I got it out this year to use as a Bimini, there were some very weird stains on the windows that I could not remove. We sailors just cannot win. Hence off to the repair shop.

Mary decided that as we were getting older and as Siobhan had made a comment about how hard it is to sit for long periods on hard teak cockpit seats, that we should try to be more accommodating to our guests, and that we needed were some cockpit cushions "just like everyone else". While I could not see the point, sometimes it is politic to give in gracefully, it was only money and I could not take it with me. So it was done.

It was after this that we heard we had three days to get back to the UK before we would be locked in for fourteen days as our Prime Minister had just removed Portugal from the Covid safe places list.

We left Lagos for the airport in Faro by Taxi the following day with sad hearts, but at least we had experienced an adventure with Dofesaba II, unlike many of our friends who had not felt safe leaving England. We counted ourselves blessed. Our adventures for 2020 were over. We have no idea what 2021 will bring, or even if we will be allowed to leave UK. Look out for our next 'Adventures', on a good internet site near you.

Figure 77 From Isla Cristina to Lagos

Some End of Season Statistics

Total Miles travelled	354.5
Fuel used	~200 L/€220
Engine Hours	55
Hours under way	70.0
Sailing hours	21.5 = 31%
Ports/Marinas visited	18
Anchorages	1
Days on Boat	54
Visitors to Boat	3

Note : All pictures taken with an iPhone7 copyright PJBell. All maps from Google Earth.

Figure 78 The whole journey 2020

Glossary of Terms in Alphabetical order.

AIS – Automatic Identification System a VHF GPS Satellite based system mandatory on all ships over 300 tons. A good idea for sailing vessels which are small, unreflective and so more difficult to see on Radar Very handy.

Bimini – Canvas shelter on the back of the boat that connects with the sprayhood to give shelter from the sun to the whole cockpit. Allows you to drive without being burned.

Boom Boom – a very British way of indicating that a joke had been told. Comes directly from a catchphrase from Basil Brush – (you will have to look that one up.)

Brighton – a seaside resort closest to London. Capital of the artistic and gay communities. Site of the first nudists beach in the UK (1979)

A Brompton – British made folding bicycles, very light, very robust, very expensive. Popular with British cruising sailors. The wheels are only sixteen inches in diameter.

Cabo de Gato - The Cape of the Cat. Another of these "ooooh you better be careful there" places which, if taken in reasonable weather with the correct tide and a good lookout, is not too bad. Also contains the local Spanish Coastguard base.

Calle – Spanish for small Bay often, but not necessarily with a small sandy beach at its head. Can be a shelter if facing the right direction. Caused by a crack or fissure within the local rock and then weathered

Code Zero – A large sail, bigger than a genoa and smaller than a gennaker. We do not have one

Competent Crew level – RYA sailing training has many levels of competence, of which Competent Crew is the first level.

Crash Gybe – When sailing downwind and the boom and/or the jib swings from all the way out on one side to all the way out on the other. This can put severe stress on the rig and can be very dangerous to the sailors in the cockpit.

A Decky – Sailors slang for a Deckhand, they do what the skipper says, are able to stand a watch and are part of a delivery crew. Usually young couples wanting a sailing adventure with a minute amount of cash thrown in.

Doris Stokes solution – Doris was a self professed spiritualist and professed to speak with the dead. She was known as 'The Happy Medium' This is a bit of a pun. The British like them.

Farewell and fair winds – Traditional Sailor's way of saying 'Good Bye'

Flogging – Sailor's slang for when a sail flaps rapidly back and forth. This is very annoying as it makes a nasty noise and can ruin the sail itself.

Force 7-8 – part of the Beaufort scale – basically very windy very bumpy and damned uncomfortable. Our boat can handle it and so can we, as we have proven several times – but it is not fun in any way. Wise skippers stay away from that.

Heaving like a good'un – putting a lot of effort into it.

To heave off/to – Verb; Sailor speak for to come to a stop.

The Iron topsail – Sailor's slang for the engine. When clipper ships wanted to get that extra speed they let loose the topsails (Along with many others)

The Island – Local way of saying 'The Isle of Wight' with Yarmouth being the other end of the Lymington-Yarmouth ferry.

Knackered – a South London expression meaning broken. Comes from when a horse was no longer able to pull a hansom cab back in Victorian times, he was sent off to the knacker's yard for converting into glue and other rendered products.

LJ – short for Life Jackets; Automatically inflating buoyancy devices designed to keep your head out of the water.

The Mark One eyeball – Sailor's slang for using your eyes and working with what you see.

Marina TV – The act of watching boats manoeuvring within a Marina in the hope that the skipper is incompetent and something exciting will happen. Often well worth the wait.

Mayday call.- a formulaic message on VHF channel 16 to let people know you are in distress and need assistance. Not to be done lightly.

OTT – Over The Top; gone a bit far; way too much.

Passerelle – French for Gangplank, used by yachties as opposed to Gangplank, as that is what pirates use and we are not pirates no matter how many flags you see. Used to be a builders plank but now far more sophisticated aluminium versions exist which fold away nicely.

Picon – French version of Angostura bitters that can be added to a pint of Lager to give it flavour. Almost makes it taste like a pint of Bitter.

To Pootle – Verb, to go forward whimsically. Slowly, without purpose or rush. Less than a trundle.

Poufter Bars – An Australian expression used to describe extra handholds so that one did not miss one's step in a bouncing cockpit.

The Punic Coast – The East coast of Spain, called after the Punic wars between Roman Empire and the Carthaginian Empire 264-146 BC. The area of Spain (Hispania) that was wrestled from Carthaginian control by Rome.

The Red Duster – Navy slang for the British red ensign, slightly disrespectful as all British Navy ships fly the white ensign.

Ria – Similar to a Calle but actually a sunken river valley often with beaches on the sides as opposed to the head – see Cornwall.

The Rias (of NE Spain) – a beautiful cruising ground very sheltered, with many Natural and National Parks. Lots of places for enjoying a holiday in. Ideal for lifting keel yachts like ours. Easy to get to from UK. Also known as part of Galicia.

RIB – Rigid Inflatable Boat. Usually with a hard floor, with two inflatable tubes either side and a very large outboard motor on the back. Goes fast, doesn't have any sails – so a bit pointless.

Sevriano Ballesteros – World Champion Golfer – reckoned to be the Greatest Continental European golfer of all time. He was Spanish

Sherbets – English slang for a drink, usually alcoholic

Singapore in 1941 – At the start of WWII the British upgraded Singapore harbour with massive 15 inch naval guns and lots of extra emplacements so as to be able to ward off any invading forces. Unfortunately no-one told the Japanese who refused to play the game properly and invaded from the North on bicycles pedalling undetected through the jungle catching the base totally by surprise.

Slight chop. – Chop is an expression for small confused waves not coming from any one specific direction. Solent chop is well known and can cause sea sickness.

South West Trains – The overground train company that serves er... the South West of the UK. Hopefully soon to be integrated back into the National British Rail.

The Stand On vessel. – According to the IALA rules, the vessel that has right of way, albeit both vessels have a duty not to collide.

Mr Sulu - a Star Trek helmsman, "Full reverse thrusters" was shouted at him when the Starship Enterprise was heading into danger.

Sun over the yardarm – a naval expression based on square rigged ships. From the quarterdeck, where the officers stood, if the angle of the sun was such that it was below the level of the yardarm – which is the large horizontal "yard" supporting the top of the mainsail, then it was late enough in the afternoon to have a drink. So time for a sherbet.

There's the rub – a Shakespearian expression (Hamlet: in the "To be or not to be" soliloquy) a rub is a flaw, as in a surface or a plan.

To T-Bone another boat – to hit them in the side creating 2 right angles either side of your prow / Sharp End. If two fibre glass boats hit, the sharp end of one is flattened and it creates a hole in the side of the other. If either are made of stronger stuff (Wood/Steel/Concrete) then a more obvious disaster can occur. A manoeuvre to be avoided at all costs.

To Troll – Verb, to wander slowly yet purposefully – similar to pootle but slightly more forcefully.

To Trundle - Verb - to go forward steadily, not fast and not erratically.

A Wee taddy – a very small amount

To Whinge – Australian slang for to Complain.

Printed in the United States
By Bookmasters